diversity and the church

diversity and the church
a search for dignity in the household of god

Based on

THE ISSUE OF ETHNICITY IN THE KOREAN-AMERICAN CHURCH: A STUDY OF AN ENGLISH-SPEAKING CONGREGATION

by

James Andrew Lee

A Final Project Report
Submitted to the Faculty of
Princeton Theological Seminary
in Partial Fulfillment of
the Requirement for
the Degree of Doctor of Ministry

Princeton, New Jersey
May 1999

To my children, Tim and Candy,
who are increasingly at home
being both ethnic and multicultural.

table of contents

endorsement

Diversity and the Church by Rev. James A. Lee is an outstanding book written from his many years of pastoral experience and extensive research. He provides in-depth analyses of the common struggles of the diaspora churches, particularly Korean-American churches, which need to adjust for multiple cultures, languages and generations. Next, he offers solutions to prevent the Silent Exodus from the mother church, or from the Christian faith itself. This study provides several guiding principles for Asian-American and Korean-American church leaders who are intent on fulfilling the Great Commission and playing a role in the Kingdom expansion of Jesus Christ. It is my sincere desire that this book will give hope and instruction to many pastors, missionaries, and serious disciples of Christ to reach the unchurched.

Won Sang Lee, Ph. D.

President of SEED International

Senior Pastor Emeritus
Korean Central Presbyterian Church
Centreville, VA

foreword

I have known James since our days at Westminster Theological Seminary back in 1987. I have watched him struggle through deep theological issues as a student, take on pastoral leaderships in various Korean-American churches, found and lead a mission organization in China back when it was rare and even dangerous to do missions work there, and plant an English-speaking church for second and third generation Chinese immigrants living in Los Angeles. This is to say that James' experiences in the field of ethnic church dynamics is both deep and wide, and it makes him a very creditable author on the subject.

Having ministered in ethnic churches through most of my 27-year pastorate in America (I now pastor in Korea), I had to ask hard questions regarding the validity of our existence. There is definitely a need for ethnic churches to serve the spiritual needs of its constituents, but is there a need for such fellowship beyond the first generation? Even if the succeeding generations, who no longer have linguistic and cultural inhibitions their parents often experienced, choose to fellowship at ethnic congregations for variety of reasons, does this ultimately honor the cause of Christ who prayed for unity among His followers? These weren't just practical questions, they were existential in nature. At least it was for me.

I came to discover that one of the most important reasons for the continuation of ethnic churches in America was to reignite spiritual fervency in the landscape of the American church. While the non-ethnic churches in America were generally declining in terms of number and commitment, churches of Latin, African, and Asian origin were vibrant and continued to grow. And these churches were infusing renewed spiritual vigor to the whole of society, which had gone distinctly secular. Here was the wisdom of God! He had allowed ethnic churches to form and grow beyond the years of their founding generations so that the spiritual dynamism in America would not wane. This understanding then became a foundation from which I began a "3 generation movement," along the teaching of Joel 2:28, where the spiritual dynamism of the father/first generation would be handed down to the next generation. If God is using the dynamics of the first-generation spirituality to bless the land, then it becomes imperative for the next generation to observe, learn, and ultimately take the baton themselves and continue the good fight.

What I've tried to explain above is just one pastor's struggle to comprehend his calling to serve at an ethnic church. However, I believe this question is being wrestled in the minds and hearts of many tens of thousands of God's servants laboring for the Gospel in ethnic congregations. For such servants of the Lord, this book will be a breath of fresh air and an arsenal of new insights. But I believe the value of this book will go much further. If the Lord is indeed using the immigrant churches in America to reawaken the lost spirituality of this land, then the lessons found in this book will encourage readers of all backgrounds. And if the world at large has now become thoroughly cosmopolitan, then churches of any nation will have to ponder the issues of multi-ethnic outreach and church planting. I pray that the church of our Lord Jesus Christ will deeply think through this issue and come out of it more refined and vibrant.

Daniel SungWook Kim

Senior Pastor
Hallelujah Community Church, Bundang, Korea

Former Senior Pastor
Sarang Community Church, Anaheim, CA

preface

American churches in general, and ethnic churches in particular, are engaged in an intense debate over ethnic diversity. In order to better understand the issues involved and examine the people's perception of ethnic ministry in an increasingly multiethnic society, a study of ethnic churchgoers was conducted.

The working theory that "most English-speaking adult ethnic Christians first look at ethnicity when selecting a church" was tested. To do this, a 250-member English-speaking Asian congregation in the metropolitan DC area was selected and surveyed. The survey content and wording were based on the results of two focus groups of church attendees convened to identify a variety of thoughts, feelings, and positions at work in the issue of ethnicity. Upon approval by the faculty advisors, Drs. Geddess Hanson and Sang Hyun Lee of Princeton Seminary, the survey was administered to the whole congregation.

One finding which quickly became a focal point was the discrepancy between the respondents' stated main reasons for choosing a church and their perception of others' reasons for the choice. The largest number of respondents believed that most English-speaking ethnics look at ethnicity first in church selection while most of the respondents themselves claimed reasons other than ethnicity.

However, a careful analysis of the results of the entire survey seems to indicate that the respondents also look at ethnicity first. There seems to be a suppression or at least self-misconception of one's own desire for ethnic comfort zone

Evidence for differences of opinions between male and female, single and married, ethnic and non-ethnic, and bilingual and monolingual members was carefully analyzed and studied.

A more thorough study of the apparent ethnic denial of the need for a personal ethnic comfort zone is in order. A competent understanding of the "mind" of the English-speaking ethnics in the area of ethnicity and an appropriate ministerial response will contribute to determining the spiritual and numerical growth of the ethnic English-language churches.

acknowledgements

From early in my days at Westminster Theological Seminary, some fellow seminarians and I debated the future of the immigrant church. We covered a wide range of issues, from generational conflicts to multiculturalism. Sometimes we talked all night, examining where our beloved church was and pondering where it might be going.

Our debates were interesting and lively, but I always lamented the fact that there was virtually no scholarly research on the subject, leaving little room for more than conjecture or partisan expression. I wanted more and better for my church community.

This desire was heightened when I became involved with an English-language ministry at a church in Philadelphia and increased more when I began my first formal adult English-language ministry at the Presbyterian Church of the Palisades (aka Living Hope Church) in Old Tappan, New Jersey.

Ministering at these churches, I began to see that ethnicity as an issue was tearing many ethnic English-language ministries apart. I realized, furthermore, that unless the immigrant church deals with the issue biblically and sensitively, the future of the ethnic English-language ministries would be in doubt. These realizations and others like them led me to this study and the research described herein.

There are many without whose support this project would not have been possible. At the top of the list is my dear wife, Soo. Ever since we decided to enter ministry together over a twenty-five years ago, she has been unswerving in her dedication to Christ and love for the people of God. Without her consistent prayers and sacrificial support, this project would not have been possible. I am deeply grateful to her for believing in me and sharing the same vision for the project.

I also thank the leadership of the Korean Central Presbyterian Church's English Ministry (aka Christ Central Presbyterian Church). Their support with intangibles like prayer and encouragement and with tangibles such as a scholarship and study-leaves has enabled me to finish these studies much more quickly than otherwise. Regular members of the English-speaking congregation have been very gracious in supporting the project by providing new insights, participating in the survey, and otherwise helping. One person to whom I am very grateful is David Linton who proofread the text and offered valuable suggestions. He and others have been sources of inspiration.

With this in mind, it seemed best to dedicate this work to the English-speaking congregation of the Korean Central Presbyterian Church and all the future generations they represent. May God use this work to build up the church for his glory. May God raise up this and future generations to reach out to every unreached people group—to the glory of the Father, Son, and the Holy Spirit. Maranatha!

section one

the ethnic

introduction

To Be or Not to Be

Many ethnic churches in America are embroiled in debate over the state and direction of its ministry, which while predominant one ethnicity, is becoming ever more diverse. There is much disagreement about where that diversity is headed and where it *should* head. The disagreement is most acute among the growing English-language ministries within the immigrant mother churches, due to the English-speaking generation's greater degree of exposure to an increasingly multicultural and multiethnic society.

The division of opinion forms a spectrum of views on how ethnic or multiethnic congregations should exist within the English-speaking ethnic church.[1] On one extreme, a very small minority wants to hold tenaciously to an exclusively ethnic English language ministry.[2] On the other extreme, others desire a multiethnic ministry devoid of ethno-cultural nuances.

Many ethnic churchgoers hold to one or the other of these views. However, there is a third, undersubscribed view that should be explored and refined. Although a church must be ethnically inclusive

---

[1] Some terms need to be defined at this point. When this report mentions "English-speaking congregation", a dependent or semi-independent daughter church within the mother church is meant.

[2] When English-speaking or language ministry is mentioned, it is meant to describe both a daughter church within a mother church and an independent English-speaking church unless specifically defined.

to be genuinely Christian, it is equally critical (and absolutely biblical) that there be minority cultural ministries.

The view espoused in this report is of churches that are culturally specific but ethnically inclusive. The starting point of the discussion is ethno-cultural identity, which is examined herein through a working theory that states: "Most English-speaking ethnic churchgoers look at ethnicity first when selecting a church."

Initial data collected from one English-speaking ethnic congregation seems to confirm the working theory while also revealing an apparent reluctance of English-speaking ethnics to admit their desire to be ministered to in a culturally relevant setting. While describing the congregation's views on ethnic issues, this report also outlines the apparent unconscious suppression of individual admissions of ethno-cultural needs in the church. A hypothesis will be suggested for further exploration of the "mind" of the English-speaking ethnic Christian who struggles in the wilderness of inbetweenness and marginality in a society, which is still racially and ethnically divided.

Balkanization of America

Some have said that the eleven o'clock hour on Sunday morning is the most segregated time in America. Most churches in the US are very ethnically or racially divided, and this is especially conspicuous during this popular worship time. Despite the fact that nearly every major institution in the US is broadly integrated, this is not so for most churches. Workplaces and friendships may be multiethnic, but spiritual homes are still predominantly white, black, Asian or Hispanic.

The segregation of churches in the US is not only true at the level of the individual congregation, but also at the national, denominational level. Even after three hundred years, the Reformed denominations are still more or less Dutch, the Evangelical Free Church is Swedish, Lutherans are German, Presbyterians are Scotch-Irish, and Baptist and Methodists are Anglo-Saxon. When one looks at the walls of division between white churches ethnically, one wonders if there will ever be a time when blacks, Asians, and whites are able to worship together without feeling uncomfortable. Whether one likes it or not, ethnicity and Christianity are inseparably intertwined. Martin Marty has said it well when he pointed out:

> Ethnicity is the skeleton of religion in America because it provides the supporting frame-work, the bare outlines or main features of American religion.[3]

An Ethnic Church[4]

---

[3] Fumitaka Matsuoka, Out of Silence: *Emerging Themes in Asian American Churches* (United Church Press, 1995), 13, citing Martin E. Marty, *Religion and Republic: The American Circumstance* (Boston: Beacon Press, 1987), 231.

[4] In this report, the Korean-American Church and Korean churches in America are one and the same. They both describe churches which are predominantly Korean, whether Korean-speaking or English speaking.

The approximately 4,500 Korean churches in North America are no exception.[5] The majority is both Korean-speaking and Presbyterian.[6] The church is ethnically homogeneous and, as with other ethnic groups in the US, there is a dominant denomination associated. Observing this phenomenon, Professor Leonora Tubbs-Tisdale at Princeton Theological Seminary says:

> Focusing upon four societal divisions—class, race, national origin, and regionalism— Niebuhr demonstrated the primacy of these

---

[5] At the time of this report, there were about 3,000. See *Korean Church Directory of North America* (The Korean Christian Press, 1997). To be precise, 2,813 churches are listed in the directory. In 2012 there were about 4,500 Korean churches in North America. http://www.koreadaily.com/news/read.asp?art_id=1569906 (accessed January 9, 2014). According to 2009 data, out of about 7,000 Asian-American churches in the US, there were about 4,000 Korean-American churches, more than all the other Asian-American churches combined. What happens to the Korean-American church will probably affect the rest of the Asian-American Christians. See http://l2foundation.org/2009/how-many-asian-american-churches-in-the-usa (accessed January 9, 2014). Asian-American seminary graduates are also overwhelmingly Korean. A consequence of such numerical strength can be seen in the number of pastors that Korean-American churches provide for English-speaking Asian churches in the US. This means, Korean-American spirituality will undoubtedly affect the future of the Asian-American church.

[6] Milton J. Coalter, John M. Mulder, and Louis b. Weeks, eds. *The Diversity of Discipleship: Presbyterians and Twentieth-Century Christian Witness* (Westminster/John Knox Press, 1991), 321. More recent data shows 58.3% as Presbyterians, the next biggest at 9.4% as Baptists, and 6.9% as Methodists. http://usaamen.net/news/board.php?board=njnews&sort=wdate&command=body&no=352 (accessed January 9, 2014)

factors in shaping America's denominational life.[7]

However, for the Korean-Americans in particular and the Asian-Americans in general, denominational loyalty is becoming less important, as the English-speakers find only a handful of ethnic churches that provide English-language services and ministry. As long as English-speakers[8] can find a church where they feel at home, denominationalism seems to have become less relevant to them.

In this sense, English-speaking Asians are like the mainstream Anglo Christians. With the erosion of denominational and other affiliative ties, [9] the mainstream American Christians also increasingly seek

---

[7] Leonora Tubbs-Tisdale, *Preaching as Local Theology and Folk Art* (Augsburg Fortress, 1997), 14, citing H. Richard Niebuhr, *The Social Sources of Denominationalism* (Henry Holt, 1929).

[8] There are many ways to categorize Koreans living in America. Some have used "first generation" as denoting the Korean-speaking group and "second generation" as the English-speaking group within the Korean community in the US. However, because of the presence of the third generation, and the so-called 1.5 generation (I prefer the term bilingual) who were born in Korea but having immigrated at an early age, are primarily English-speakers; the aforementioned generational terms are inaccurate and inadequate. Therefore, a different term is used in this report. There are among Koreans, regardless of generational affiliation, those who prefer to function in an English-speaking group. This group, which I call "the English-speaking Koreans or English-speaking Korean-Americans, includes 1.5 (bilingual), second, third and even a small number of first generation Korean-Americans.

[9] Robert Wuthnow, *The Restructuring of American Religion: Society and Faith since World War II* (Princeton University Press, 1988), 71-99.

congregations where they are 'at home" or feel that they "belong."[10] To Anglos the most important factor in choosing a church that gives them a sense of belonging may be cultural relevance in a generational way (i.e. boomer or Generation X), for they often do not have to actively search for predominantly white churches. On the other hand, English-speaking Asians, while also seeking cultural relevance in a generational way, are compelled to look harder for churches that provide ethno-cultural relevance.[11]

In addition to the increasingly prevalent non-denominationalism at work in the English-speaking ethnics in America, as more independent English-speaking churches and adult congregations within the mother church structure are established, the issue of ethnicity becomes more and more prominent in the discussion among the church leaders, as well as members. This is especially true as the society as a whole and the English-speaking ethnic churches become more multiethnic—unlike the immigrant mother churches, which cannot accommodate non-ethnics due to the language barrier.

---

[10] Leonora Tubbs-Tisdale, *Preaching as Local Theology and Folk Art* (Augsburg Fortress, 1997), 15.

[11] This is also true of Korean-speaking churchgoers in the US. At any given Korean church in the US, one will find Presbyterians, Methodists, Baptists, Pentecostals, and others in its congregation. The congregational make up is even more complicated by the presence of people who are prone to regional animosities and people from different socio-economic ladder. This multi-denominational, multi-regional and multi-socio-economic mix is probably due to lack of church choice among Koreans in America. In Korea, churches are more or less grouped along denominational, regional and socio-economic lines.

Thus, for English-speaking ethnics, there are two major elements that are in tension in their approach to ministry. First, most of them seem to want culturally relevant ministry. But their need for cultural relevancy conflicts with the second element, a desire to be inclusive ethnically. In other words, it is apparent that they do not want to give up their specialized ministry that caters to English-speaking ethnics, but their distaste for ethnocentrism and ethnic isolationism seems to compel them to suppress any hint of an overt display of ethnic culture and pride in ministry, especially in the Asian context. They seem to want to avoid alienation of their non-ethnic friends in church as well as potential new non-ethnic members.[12] As Karen Chai concludes in her research:

> English-speaking Koreans look for a church that is inviting and open to non-Koreans and facilitates Korean-Americans' expression of their ethnic identity.[13]

In the end, however, most English-speaking ethnic congregations and churches usually opt for a superficial elimination of all ethnic elements (e.g. language, cultural practices, etc.) in the official

---

[12] According to the Final Project survey results, most non-Koreans do not object to the practice of Korean cultural elements in the church or the inclusion of "Korean' in the church name. It is the English-speaking Koreans who seem to be more sensitive about them. They seem to be very conscious of the presence of non-Koreans in the congregation and want to go out of their ways to cater to them. See Appendix One #13 and Appendix Two #13.

[13] R. Stephen Warner and Judith G. Wittner, eds. *Gathering in Diaspora: Religious Communities and the New Immigration* (Temple University Press, 1998), 304.

ministry functions except the human faces. This practice is informal but pervasive; although nearly all ethnic English-language congregations and churches quietly and unofficially reach out to an ethnically narrow constituency, few specifically state this in their mission statements.[14]

This tension seems to be almost ubiquitous in the Asian-American church. The members within the church can be grouped broad into two: First is the "ethnocentrists" who unswervingly advocate particularly ethnic ministries in the US. The second group is the "non-ethnicists" who despite having chosen to attend an ethnic church, prefer toning down or even totally eliminating all ethnic elements in the church. They sometimes resemble those who advocate multiethnic church but the major difference is their decision to attend an ethnic church. The fundamental disagreement between the two groups begins at the theological level and the following is a gist of the debate.

---

[14] There is one church in Manhattan, Korean Methodist Church and Institute, whose English ministry is unapologetically Korean in orientation as of 1999. The church has been known for its aggressive ethno-political and cultural agenda which goes back almost eighty years. But in 2014, even this church has dropped the Korean-specific vision statement. Until recently, the mission statement of Korean Central Presbyterian Church's English Ministry (aka Christ Central Presbyterian Church) specifically stated that they exist to reach out to those who identify with the Korean –American culture.

chapter one

theological debate

Jesus and the Disciples

Advocates of the melting pot church model point to many passages in the Bible to justify their claim that such churches are the only biblically legitimate model. In other words, it is absolutely unchristian for Christians who are supposedly redeemed by the blood of Christ to gather into enclaves because of ethnic and racial differences and not unite with one another. They say that it is understandable when this happens as a result of language and geopolitical barriers, but when there is no such division in a single society that is pluralistic ethnically but shares a common language, it borders on apostasy. Assimilationists frown upon such division as totally unbiblical and offer evidence such as that propounded by A.B. Bruce. He writes that Jesus intentionally chose a diverse group of individuals among his disciples so that they would learn how to become an interdependent community:

> It gives one a pleasant surprise to think of Simon the zealot and Matthew the publican, men coming from so opposite quarters, meeting together in close fellowship in the little band of the twelve. In the persons of these two disciples extremes meet—the tax-gatherer and the tax-hater; the unpatriotic Jew, who degraded himself by becoming a servant

11

of the alien ruler; and the Jewish patriot, who chafed under foreign yoke, and sighed for emancipation. This union of opposites was not accidental, but was designed by Jesus as a prophecy of the future.[15]

However, Peter Wagner notes, in contrast, that Jesus discipled his followers in an ethnically homogeneous unit.[16] All but one of them were Jews and from the region of Galilee. In fact, the one who was non-Galilean, from "Cariot" or "Iscariot", betrayed Jesus. Thus, it is undeniable that Jesus' disciples were diverse socio-politically but not ethnically, apparently to give cohesive culture and unity to the group.

The Early Church

Proponents of multiethnic ministry also argue that Acts 13:1 shows the church in Antioch as multiethnic. The passage says, "in the church at Antioch there were prophets and teachers: Barnabas, Simeon called Niger, Lucius of Cyrene, Manaen and Saul" The advocates of the multiethnic church model assert that the presence of Simeon called Niger in the church tells us that at least one of the leaders was a black African and thus the church was multiethnic.

Here, two things are assumed without solid evidence. The first is that a nickname positively confirms the ethnicity of the person (But he could have

---

[15] A.B. Bruce, *The Training of the Twelve* (Kregel, 1971), 35-36.
[16] C. Peter Wagner, *Our Kind of People: The Ethnic Dimensions of Church Growth in America* (John Knox Press, 1979), 4.

12

been a dark-skinned Jew who in fact had a Hebrew name). The second is that there was a mega-church that met at one place in Antioch instead of small house churches.

According to Wagner, this scenario is unlikely. The Church in Antioch more likely resembled a presbytery (a fellowship of local churches) than a mega-church, and it probably had many house churches of diverse ethnic composition. We cannot know for certain how they were organized, but these house churches were probably not uniform throughout. Some were probably multiethnic, some predominantly Jewish and others predominantly Greek.

Galatians 3:28

Another passage often cited by the proponents of multiethnic ministry is Galatians 3:28: "There is neither Jew nor Greek, slave nor free, male nor female, for you are all one in Christ Jesus." This passage seems to mandate multiethnic, classless and unisex churches. However, when one looks at the context of this and many other related passages, the message of the texts is not multiethnic ministry. The Galatians passage, for example, is addressing the *legitimacy* of the multiple ethnic approach to the gospel. The Epistle was Paul's polemic against the dominant culture (in this case, Jewish), which threatened the legitimacy of the minority (Greek) interpretation and application of the gospel. He basically says that if anyone absolutizes a culture and makes it a prerequisite to salvation, he or she is preaching a different gospel and must be condemned. Paul, in effect, is saying to the Judaizers to let the gentiles or Greeks be saved by grace in their own cultural way, not through Jewish religio-cultural rituals.

While Paul does condemn the Jews for imposing their culture on the gentiles, he never condemned the Jews for practicing the gospel according to their own context. As Brett succinctly points out:

> Paul does not erase or eradicate cultural specificities but relativizes them. No one culture is despised or demonized or absolutized or allowed hegemony."[17]

In other words, Paul saw the body of Christ consisting of all peoples of the earth, but did not try to subordinate gentile culture under the patron culture of the Jews.

Contextualization

In modern times, this espousing of alternative interpretation and application with a certain degree of independence from the dominant culture is called "contextualization." In other words, a minority culture is encouraged to interpret the Bible in light of its own cultural and historical context thus developing its own distinct indigenous theology. Interpretation gives us "theology." Application makes it "ethnic". [18] When Asian-Americans apply the Bible in their life situations, we call it Asian-American theology. A good example

---

[17] Mark G Brett, *Ethnicity and the Bible* (E.J. Brill 1996), 211.
[18] Harvie M. Conn, *Eternal Word and Changing Worlds: Theology, Anthropology, and Mission in Trialogue* (Zondervan, 1984), 122.

of this is the theology of "marginality" in the Asian Christian community in North America.[19]

On the other hand, some conservative, mainstream Christians, having been marginalized by the secular world into roles that are increasingly less influential, have contextualized their experience of marginality into a theology of reconstruction base on theonomy.[20] To them, the glory days of cultural dominance of the church can return by Christianizing the secular culture. To an Asian-American like myself, however, who come from a culture where the church has never been dominant, the whole debate is less meaningful: The Asian church has been for most part pre-Constantinian, and the mainstream post-Constantinian struggle is but

---

[19] The theology of marginality is an attempt at contextualization of the minority American experience, particularly that of Asian-Americans who feel they are in-between, at the periphery of, or even outside the mainstream American public life. However, instead of becoming invisible or "nothing" in the eyes of the dominant culture, Asian-Americans creatively become simultaneously transcendent and immanent of both Asian and American cultures and form a creative core apart from the real core of the mainstream America. Through the example of Christ, the ultimate marginal man, who was cast out by the mainstream Jewish society, Asian-Americans seek to embrace all humanity who are blind and limited in perspective due to their over-immersion into one narrow experience, into a new humanity. See Jung Young Lee, *Marginality: The Key to Multicultural Theology* (Augsburg Fortress, 1995).

[20] Theonomy, also known as Christian Reconstructionism, posits that the biblical law is applicable to civil law, and proposes biblical law as the standard by which the laws of nations may be measured, and to which they ought to be conformed.

a distant struggle between the hostile secular culture and the increasingly alienated Western church.[21]

Therefore, for theology to be relevant and helpful to Americans in general and minorities in particular, Asian-Americans must be encouraged to formulate their own personal response to the gospel call. This happens when they are encouraged to be nurtured in a culturally relevant ministry context. Contextualization is critical because theology always shapes the life, faith and practice of the believer. A theology that lacks relevance helps the believer very little. It may even be harmful. As Samuel Ling advocates:

> Through the theology of culture, each cultural group must be encouraged to inquire into the justification for and the process in expressing and applying the gospel in a particular cultural context, which is sometimes called indigenization or contextualization.[22]

Without a church that inculcates ethnic dignity, even greater numbers of the unchurched ethnics will be forever lost to the dark world without Christ. Furthermore, they will fail to heed the divine call to

---

[21] Pre-Constantinian means the church before Constantine, which was persecuted by the dominant pagan society. Post-Constantinian means the church that has lost its influence in the secular society. As a pre-Constantinian church, Asian churches have rarely had a problem of power struggle against the state. So, not being able to pray in public schools at graduation ceremonies or not being able to set up a nativity scene in front of the city hall does not seem to bother them as much.

[22] Cecilia Yau, ed. *A Winning Combination: ABC/OBC: Understanding the Cultural Tensions in Chinese Churches* (Chinese Christian Mission, 1986), 74.

contribute to the mosaic of world Christianity enough to make a meaningful difference in the world. It is imperative that strategic and systematic methods be employed to win the souls of the marginalized for the Kingdom of God. The words of Paul are a poignant reminder that providing a relevant gospel message to the believer and unbeliever alike is critical to the preservation and expansion of God's Kingdom on earth:

> To the Jews I became like a Jew, to win the Jews. To those under the law I became like one under the law, so as to win those under the law. To those not having the law I became like one not having the law, so as to win those not having the law. To the weak I became weak, to win the weak. I have become all things to all men so that by all possible means I might save some. I do all this for the sake of the gospel, that I may share in its blessings. (I Corinthians 9:20-23)

The message of Paul is clear. One must cater to the needs and sensitivities of particular ethnic (thus the Jews), religious (those under the law), and many other groups in the society so that the gospel can be heard by everyone without hindrance. In other words, it is absolutely biblical and Christian to have special churches and missionary organizations that reach out to the Jews, Muslims, English-speaking Koreans, and others so that all these will become part of the greater Kingdom of God.

Church Catholic and Local Church

No one can ignore, however, that the Scriptures teach the collective unity of the church. In other words, it is equally Christian and biblical to believe that the church is one and universal, as can be seen in a biblical vision of a multiethnic heavenly worship:

> After this I looked and there before me was a great multitude that no one could count, from every nation, tribe, people and language, standing before the throne and in front of the Lamb. They were wearing white robes and were holding palm branches in their hands. And they cried out in a loud voice:
>
>> "Salvation belongs to our God,
>> who sits on the throne,
>> and to the Lamb." (Revelation 7:9)

This is John's description of the heavenly assembly worshipping God. It's fully multiethnic. This indeed is the church catholic (universal), the invisible church as God sees it. The Bible teaches that there is only one church, as Jesus says in Matthew 16:18: "…on this rock I will build my church…" And in this church are the elect from every tribe and tongue, constituting the one and only body of Christ.

This fundamental unity in the midst of diversity can be seen in Paul's first letter to the Corinthians. Paul rebukes the schismatics in the Corinthian church who were forming cliques by asking a rhetorical question: "Is Christ divided?" (I Corinthians 1:13). In other words, just as Christ has one body that cannot be divided, so does the church of Christ. Paul exhorts the believers in the church to agree with one another so that there may be no division and that there may be perfect unity in mind and thought (I Corinthians 1:10).

Jesus also taught unity in the church. Christ prays to the Father in John 17:22, "I have given them the glory that you gave me, that they may be one as we are one." Here the unity of the godhead is not one of absolute oneness but collective. Jesus is one with the Father in the sense that there is only one God. However, Jesus is never lost in the godhead as a non-person. Jesus is a unique person in the godhead with all the unique attributes of a God-Man.

The Trinity gives us a unique insight into the relationship between the church catholic and the local church. Both the Trinity and the Church are of spiritual relationship and therefore share many common relational attributes. Just as the godhead is one and many, so is the Church one and many. In the church catholic, there is spiritual unity in mind and thought among believers. This enables Christians from one culture to travel to a foreign land with a totally different culture and worship together with people they do not know and still feel a strong sense of fraternity and unity.

Ultimately, unity does not conflict with diversity. The church is one, but each distinct ethnic and cultural group is given the divine approval to be ministered to in a culturally relevant way. This is the reason why the Ecumenical Council of Jerusalem recorded in Acts 15 did not require of gentiles Jewish religio-cultural practices. This is the reason why Paul preached to the Athenians by using various quotes from pagan Greek philosophers and sages in Acts 17.

Moreover, even though most Greeks and Hebrews outside Palestine could communicate through the then lingua franca, *Koine Greek*, in the local church, Paul was designated as an apostle to the gentile and Peter as an apostle to the Jew (Galatians 2:2) perhaps because their cultures were radically different despite the fact that they lived in a common Hellenistic world.

As John's vision showed, multitudes of ethnic groups will be preserved and represented in the Kingdom of God from different parts of the world. In these settings where people groups are divided by geography and language, it is natural to have ethnic churches. However, in a multicultural society like America, which shares a common language, the division seems very bothersome to a lot of Christians.

What many overlook is that speaking a common language does not mean that the people share a common culture. African-Americans, Hindu-Americans, Irish-Americans and Korean-Americans all speak English but do not share a common culture. This is why America is called a multicultural society.

Not only are there cultural differences, there are also ethnic and racial differences. Speaking the same language does not mean that everyone looks the same. Because of these differences, minorities have been traumatized by the systematic racial discrimination of the mainstream society. Therefore, many marginalized find it hard to have personal dignity in the mainstream churches. As a result, many minorities seek culturally and ethnically relevant ministries, and Asians are no exception.

Effective spiritual nurture often times requires socio-cultural relevancy. This is so because spirituality is a very personal and intimate aspect of in the life a Christian. When one receives spiritual nurture, one's most intimate secrets and needs are exposed. With such deep vulnerability, the safest environment in which one can be ministered to without misunderstanding or judgment is a place where one feels at home. To most Americans, a place where they feel safe and at home is a church full of people who share a common collective experience. This is why many white boomers look for generational churches and minorities ethnic churches. Karen Chai puts this need succinctly:

> ...the first generation is forced to choose the ethnic church, but the second generation makes the choice not because it has no other options but because the church is a safe space where ethnicity and spirituality merge into one.[23]

The Christian church must work to the best of its ability to bring unity and reconciliation both in mind and body. At the same time, specific people groups must be identified and given the opportunity to respond to the gospel and be nurtured further in a culturally safe and sensitive environment. These two biblical mandates must be addressed simultaneous on all levels of ecumenical, denominational and local fellowship. As Garriott points out:

> We shall see that the Scriptures subordinate neither the aggressive evangelism of people groups nor the reconciliation of alienated

---

[23] R. Stephen Warner and Judith G. Wittner, eds. *Gathering in Diaspora: Religious Communities and the New Immigration* (Temple University Press, 1998), 311.

diverse people to one another. Both must be preserved and pursued in the Church.[24]

Now, having presented the theological debate on the issue of ethnicity in the church, we now move on to equally hotly debated sociological issues on ethnicity and church.

[24] Craig Wesley Garriott, *Growing Reconciled Communities: Reconciled Communities Mobilized for Wholistic Growth*. Unpublished D.Min. dissertation, Westminster Theological Seminary, Philadelphia, 1996, 40.

chapter two

sociological debate

Silent Exodus

So far, the results of outreach to English-speaking Asians, particularly Korean-Americans overall have not been very encouraging. There are several factors that contribute to this dismal reality. One factor is that even though there are about 4,500 Korean churches in North America, overwhelming majority of them do not have English-language worship services and to compound the problem, many church leaders do not know how to cater to their sensitivities.[25]

The sad fact is that many of the unchurched Korean-Americans do not attend Anglo churches either. There is a reason for this. According to Dr. Sang Hyun Lee of Princeton Theological Seminary:

> The second generation...by virtue of their particular situation, face a more difficult predicament than do their elders. For one thing, they are far more deeply involved in the

---

[25] According to the 2012 study of KA Christians, 12% attend churches smaller than 20, 22.3% between 21-25, 41.3% between 40-80, and 11.4% mega-churches over 3,000. This means about 75% of Korean-American Christians attend churches with less than 80 attendees, which is far too small to offer English-language services. See http://usaamen.net/news/board.php?board=njnews&sort=wdate&command=body&no=352 (accessed January 15, 2014).

white American world than is the first generation. This means that they are self-consciously aware of their marginalization much more acutely than are their parents. In face of marginality, where the Korean Americans of the first generation have their ethnic culture and community to turn to, those of the second generation cannot do so because their ethnic attachment is not strong enough. They never belonged deeply to their Korean culture or social world and, therefore, cannot return to it. They are truly in a wilderness, in the world of in-betweenness and homelessness.[26]

Many unchurched Korean-Americans apparently do not feel at home in white churches, which do not meet their special ethno-cultural needs. The Korean churches in America are not doing better either. Many Korean churches insist that the English-speakers worship in Korean and be ministered to in a very Korean way. This seems to drive the English-speakers out of their mother church. What they need is ethnically and culturally relevant English language ministries that meet their needs. The failure to provide English language ministries seems to be the biggest reason why there is a massive exodus of English-speaking Koreans from the church.

Although there are no official data on the number of English-speaking Koreans that attend church, many

---

[26] Milton J. Coalter, John M. Mulder and Louis B. Weeks, eds. *The Diversity of Discipleship: Presbyterians and Twentieth-Century Christian Witness* (Westminster/John Knox Press, 1991), 316-317.

estimate that the figure is quite low. According to some estimates, 90 percent of post-college Korean-Americans no longer attend church.[27]

This is stark contrast to one figure, which claims that 77 percent of Koreans in the US are churched.[28] Similarly, a study of Korean-Americans in the New York City area found that while up to 75 percent of the first generation attend church, only five percent of English-speaking Koreans remain in the church after college.[29] What's desperately needed are more English language churches and ministries, which provide a haven or home for the traumatized and marginalized Korean-Americans. A need for home is true to all people:

> A significant number of African-Americans and Hispanics have moved into a middle class that is not always at home in its former churches. This number will grow as the

---

[27] R. Stephen Warner and Judith G. Wittner, *Gatherings in Diaspora: Religious Communities and the New Immigration* (Temple University Press, 1998), 300.

[28] Harvie M. Conn, *The American City and the Evangelical Church: A Historical Overview* (Baker Books, 1994), 195, citing Yong-soo Hyun, *The Relationship Between Cultural Assimilation Models, Religiosity, and Spiritual Well-Being Among Korean-American College Students and Young Adults in Korean Churches in Southern California*, Unpublished Ed.D. dissertation, Biola University, LaMirada, Calif, 1990, 1. According to a 2012 research by Pew Research found that 71% of Korean-Americans are affiliated with Christianity.
See http://www.pewforum.org/2012/07/19/asian-americans-a-mosaic-of-faiths-overview/#christians (accessed January 15, 2014)

[29] R. Stephen Warner and Judith G. Wittner, *Gatherings in Diaspora: Religious Communities and the New Immigration* (Temple University Press, 1998), 300.

middle class grows in these communities. ABC (American Born Chinese) Chinese often feel like displaced persons in churches where leadership and style are oriented to the OBC (Overseas Born Chinese) Christians. Cubans are not at home in predominantly Puerto Rican churches. Central Americans are not always comfortable in Dallas and Los Angeles churches whose constituency is largely Mexican. Vietnamese do not stay long in Cambodian-American congregations.[30]

Peter Wagner calls on us to see these different categories of ethnicity as we plot our evangelistic strategies. The sharpest ethnic distinction he calls nuclear ethnics; these will require non-English-language churches. Some are fellow-travelers or marginal ethnics and will need bilingual churches, even English-speaking Korean or Latino churches. A few are alienated ethnics, happy in Anglo churches. Dr. Harvie M. Conn of Westminster Theological Seminary adds to this list a group called cross-cultural ethnics. They find their place best in multiethnic churches.[31]

If we are to reach America's ethnic communities in the future that is already here, then, church planting must target these groups on their own contextual terms

---

[30] Harvey M. Conn, *The American City and the Evangelical Church* (Baker, 1994), 189.

[31] Ibid., 189, citing C. Peter Wagner, "A Vision for Evangelizing the Real America", *International Bulletin of Missionary Research* 10, no. 2 (April 1986): 59-64.

without forgetting the church's obligation to demonstrate its unity and catholicity.[32]

Problem of "Neutral" Culture

Another reason why even an ethnically integrated churches are not always desirable is the problem of culture. The gospel cannot be communicated without the medium of culture. In order to be effective, the gospel must be communicated in the language and culture of the people. As Niebuhr poignantly pointed out, "Man thinks and acts according to his cultural make up."[33] When someone says that all the churches ought to quit talking about culture and ethnicity and be more gospel-oriented, they forget the fact that there is no neutral culture.

Many Americans assume that the biblically normative culture in the US is the "white" culture, but in reality, the white culture is neither the most neutral nor the most Christian. There are other cultures in the US that are just as Christian. The Anglo culture might be dominant but it's hardly exclusively "Christian". The assimilationists' opposition to the ethnic churches seems to be more from American civil religion than from a purely biblical source.[34]

But dominance has its power. Thus the de facto result of calls for a multiethnic church is that most such

---

[32] Harvey M. Conn, *The American City and the Evangelical Church* (Baker, 1994), 189.

[33] H. Richard Niebuhr, *Christ and Culture* (Harper & Row, 1956), 69.

[34] C. Peter Wagner, *Our Kind of People: The Ethnic Dimensions of Church Growth in America* (John Knox Press, 1979), 53.

churches conform to the Anglo culture. The occasional exception can be seen in the few churches that use multiple languages and religio-cultural practices. [35] Even if de facto white cultural dominance can be avoided, however, another problem arises: nobody knows what a multiethnic church is! Everyone has a different definition and preference.[36]

The bottom line is without ethnic ministries, the church would not be able to effectively reach out to the lost minorities and unreached people groups in a meaningful and relevant way either in the mission field or in the home front.

Loss of Culture and Loss of Personal Dignity

For many minorities in the US, the church is the only institution in which they can raise and nurture members of their ethnic communities by inculcating distinct minority cultures, which in turn can give cohesion and meaning to their existence. Some have argued that in Christ, we have new ethnicity and old ethnicities are no longer needed. If this is true, in the same token, could a man deny his God-given sex and still be truly Christian? What would he be, a non-sexual

---

[35] Manuel Ortiz, *One New People: Models for Developing a Multiethnic Church* (InterVarsity, 1996), 52, 65, 73, 79. The churches mentioned in the pages are diverse in many ways. Some have multicultural and even multilingual services. Others are multi-congregational with ethnic pastors of their own.

[36] Manuel Ortiz, *One New People: Models for Developing a Multiethnic Church* (InterVarsity, 1996), Appendix. Five scholars were asked what multiethnic church is and all gave very different answers.

Christian who is neither male nor female? How about someone who denies himself as a member of a family? Could a person without a last name be able to function adequately as no-name Christian? Even adopted children have their adopted names and find dignity and holistic meaning as Christians with family identity. One does not become a Christian in a vacuum. The church's role is primarily spiritual, but having acknowledged that, there is no biblical grounds for condemning preservation of a marginal culture within an endangered ethnic community. Likewise, if any ethnic community loses their roots, they could lose not only dignity as persons but also the strength of their distinct moral and social fiber could be seriously compromised.

According to Mead, because of the incredibly rapid move from a cofigurative culture to a prefigurative one, certain third-world cultures, including Asian cultures, and especially Asian-American cultures, are abandoning or losing their heritage.[37] Without having a sense of identity, the members of future Asian-American generations could have difficulty as Asians, their understanding of the gospel will be less personal, if not profoundly distorted. In the worst-case scenario, utter confusion might set in.

---

[37] According to Margaret Mead, a cofigurative culture is a pre-industrialization culture that maintains its civilization by learning from peers as opposed to postfigurative culture, which maintains its society by learning from elders. As a result, its progress tends to be very slow. Prefigurative culture is the post-industrial culture in which people even learn from their children. This is possible because of the incredible amount of information that is available through modern communication network. There is a rapid change, and generation gaps become more acute within a short span of time. See Margaret Mead, *Culture and Commitment* (Doubleday, 1970).

The moral fabric of the community will begin to deteriorate, and its fate could ultimately resemble that of many displaced blacks in America and the Caribbean with their moral and social ills. To be authentic before God, Asian-Americans need to think and practice their faith in their own way. Yong Jung Lee, after quoting I Corinthians 13:11 says in his book, *Marginality*:

> Following Paul's insight, I, therefore speak like an Asian-American, I think like an Asian-American, and I reason like an Asian-American. If I don't do this, I deceive myself and my thought is not genuine.[38]

Dr. Sang Hyun Lee calls on all Asians to journey back as pilgrims to the past in order to move forward as newly empowered people of God:

> Our pilgrimage, therefore, must begin with a journey backward through time into our Asian past then proceed forward through the present to our Asian American future. All pilgrims need to make their personal time journeys back to their ethnic roots. This is true first because ethnicity is a gift of God, and second because it is a constitutive or essential element of being human. No one is just a generic human being. Each has come from a particular ethnic background. Therefore, rediscovering our Asian past and its cultural heritage is one

---

[38] Young Jung Lee, *Marginality: The Key to Multicultural Theology* (Fortress Press, 1995), 66.

concrete way in which God wants us to affirm our humanity.[39]

Vision and Identify

If the ethnic churches lose their identity, they will also be less effective in carrying out God's call to be used in a unique way. Dr. Sang Hyun Lee says:

> The creative potential of marginality has been pointed out by several important social scientists. One of them, the renowned historian Arnold Toynbee, has argued that marginal persons, having been thrown into a land of uncertainties, are forced to ask themselves who they are and what their life's meaning might be. Through such self-searching, they may emerge as persons of creative vision and energy. This sort of marginal person can truly advance human civilization and culture. Anthropologist Victor Turner calls marginality a "liminal situation" and points to its peculiar capacity to generate a genuine communion among human beings.[40]

Ethnic churches need to exist so that not only will English-speaking ethnics, such as Korean-Americans, be reached by the gospel, but the English-speaking

---

[39] Sang Hyun Lee and John V. Moore, eds. *Korean American Ministry* (PCUSA, 1993), 49-50.
[40] Ibid., 47.

Asian-Americans and furthermore all the marginalized Third World nations as well. The same could be said of the Chinese-American church or any ethnic church for that matter. This can be done only and if only English-speaking ethnics do not lose their identity as Christians and their respective culture.

"Melting Pot" versus "Stew"

Until recently, the most prevalent model of American assimilation or acculturation was the "melting-pot" model. Nativists and a substantial portion of immigrants wanted the new arrivals to be assimilated into the great American melting pot, so from many, one homogeneous group would emerge. This concept, however, is a myth and is extremely insensitive to various needs of minorities.

There is a culture in the US that identifies Christianity with Anglo-Americanism among which the Ku Klux Klan is an extreme form. This identification of Christianity with the Anglo culture finds its ultimate expression in the concepts of "Manifest Destiny" and the White Men's Burden."[41] Many Asians and Asian-Americans have bought into

---

[41] "Manifest Destiny" is a concept consisting of a peculiar mix of American civil religion and imperialism. It teaches that America has a destiny foreordained by the Supreme Being to donate North America and the Western Hemisphere and later on modified to include the rest of the world. "White Men's Burden" is a belief held by the people of European descent in which they believed that God has called them to civilize the world according to their own image.

this line of argument and have often been deprived of their authentic personhood. As Morikawa mourns:

> So thorough was the Asian capitulation, Christian conversion was equated with conversion to American values. Our journal of spiritual pilgrimage, therefore, contains dark chapters of seduction by acculturation, as a means of social and economic survival...Our ethnic language, literature, religion, culture and history, which we in our fervent efforts at acculturation deliberately rejected or ignored, is a historical treasure for us to claim, even for no other reason, than to liberate us out of our narrow American parochialism, toward a global consciousness...Thus, being who we are, creatures of the Creator God, made by Him, invisibly redeemed and reshaped by Him, conversion in Christ meant becoming who we really are in Christ, and not to become who we are not, the mythical or typical American norm.[42]

What we need at this point in our social evolution as an ethnically pluralistic society is a paradigm shift, a shift to an innovative, relevant and morally justifiable model.

Instead of melting everyone into "white" Americans, we need to uphold the dignity of different groups and form what I call a "stew" model. In it, everyone is partially melted. Not only are the smaller ingredients melted but the dominant and bigger chunks

---

[42] Jitsuo Morikawa, *Toward an Asian American Theology* (American Baptist Quarterly 12:179-186 Je 1993), 179-180.

are affected by smaller ones as well. They all evolve together. Instead of a pot with one bland flavor, diversity produces creativity, knowledge, and respect for others. Boyarin, a Jewish scholar, points out the importance of "unity in diversity" when he says:

> Somewhere in this dialectic a synthesis must be found, one that will allow for stubborn hanging on to ethnic, cultural specificity but in a context of human solidarity.[43]

Cultural Homogeneity and Church Growth

Ethnic churches are not only permissible and biblical but also imperative for the growth of churches in the US. It has often been demonstrated that churches show more vigorous growth when a homogeneous unit.[44] Whether white, black or Hispanic, churches often explode in growth when people are invited and nurtured in a setting that is safe and culturally relevant.

A church that practices this principle is Willow Creek Community Church, located in an affluent suburban setting in the Chicago metropolitan area. They are homogeneous in many ways. The church is overwhelmingly white, baby-boomer, and upper middle class. The worship style is contemporary, which attracts a younger generation. Even the church building is indicative of the mall culture of America, as it is situated on vast, park-like grounds with a lake, a food

---

[43] Mark G. Brett, *Ethnicity and the Bible* (E.J. Brill, 1996), 212.
[44] C. Peter Wagner, *Our Kind of People: The Ethnic Dimensions of Church Growth in America* (John Knox Press, 1979), 11.

court, cappuccino machines, and information monitors. The church has exploded in growth, so that after only twenty years, the average weekly attendance reached over 20,000.

A church model of culturally sensitive ministry is critical for targeting unreached people groups within the US, among which Asian-American young professionals are one of the least reached.

Transitory Nature of Multiethnic Church

One must also not forget that ethnically mixed churches are often transitory, that they are usually an interim phenomenon unless carefully balanced through strategic staff selection and target audience, which can slow down or even hamper growth. When leadership changes in a mixed church, the congregation often fragments, or one group becomes dominant over others depending often on who the pastor is.

> Circle Church…provides the example…a painful and rather abrupt split took place. The black membership and the black pastor left Circle Church and started First Corinthians Baptist church in Chicago's Austin district…The division…occurred along racial lines even though the black contingent cited problems of injustice, not racial issues.[45]

---

[45] C. Peter Wagner, *Our Kind of People: The Ethnic Dimensions of Church Growth in America* (John Knox Press, 1979), 15.

Also, Pozzetta, in his book *The Immigrant Religious Experience*, refers to a Lutheran church in Michigan, at the turn of the century in which the Swedes, Norwegians, and Finns were encouraged to join. When a Norwegian pastor of the church alienated large numbers of Finns by excommunicating them because of a religio-cultural misunderstanding, the church began to split apart. Later a new Finnish pastor, divided the congregation into three and encouraged them to worship separately. [46] The conclusion: superficial integration seldom works and can become a hindrance to evangelism and church growth. [47] The alternative is to encourage formation of local churches that can be considered home for specific groups and at the same time promote pluralism at the denomination level.[48]

Intermarriage and Assimilation

---

[46] George E. Pozzetta, *The Immigrant Religious Experience* (Garland, 1991), 355.

[47] Manuel Ortiz, *One New People: Models for Developing a Multiethnic Church* (InterVarsity, 1996), 44-62. The sample churches given in the multiethnic church models are mostly churches that do not have a dominant ethnic group within their congregations. Most of them are small churches with 100-200 members. It appears that for the sake of diversity, they have abandoned church growth and evangelism.

[48] C. Peter Wagner, *Our Kind of People: The Ethnic Dimensions of Church Growth in America* (John Knox Press, 1979), 150. Since parishioners' spiritual nurture primarily happens at a small group setting such as the local church, Wagner advocates that each church should remain more or less homogeneous but for the sake of church unity and fellowship, integration should happen at the denomination level.

Many assimilationists call for the abolition of ethnic churches by assuming that all minorities will eventually be absorbed by the dominant group. When one takes into account the intermarriage rate among Asians, this sounds all the more true. In Los Angeles County, in 1977, the marriage records indicate that 63.1 percent of Japanese, 49.7 percent of Chinese, and 34.1 percent of Koreans who married that year married outside their ethnic groups.[49] However, starting in the 1980's there has been a decrease of intermarriage in Los Angeles County. According to the Los Angeles County Marriage License Bureau, in 1984, 51.2 percent of Japanese, 30 percent of Chinese, and only 8.7 percent of Korean who married that year married outside of their ethnic groups. This decrease probably represents the growing incidence of new immigration in the Asian-American population.[50]

According to the US Census Bureau, by the year 2050, the US will have about 384 million people. Among them, roughly 52 percent will be white, 25

---

[49] Matsuoka, Fumitaka. *Out of Silence: Emerging Themes in Asian American Churches* (United Church Press, 1995), 46. The Japanese intermarriage rate in California reached the all-time high of 90% in the 80s. Some sociologists conjecture that this unusually high rate, even compared to other Asians, is due probably to the traumatic World War II concentration camp experience by the Issei and Nisei in the US. The desire to fit in seems to drive them toward total assimilation. See also Russell Endo et al, *Asian-Americans: Social and Psychological Perspective*, vol. 2 (Science and Behavior Books, 1980), 46 and Stanley Sue and James K. Morishima, *The Mental Health of Asian Americans: Contemporary Issues in Identifying and Treating Mental Problems* (Jossey-Bass, 1982), 110-111.
[50] Harry H.L. Kitano and Roger Daniels, *Asian Americans: Emerging Minorities* (Prentice Hall, 1988), 179.

percent Hispanic, 15 percent black and 8 percent Asian.[51] In other words, from the 2010 Census figure of about 17 million, there will be roughly 32-40 million Asian in the US in less than two generations. With this dramatic increase of Asian-Americans, the intermarriage rate might not dramatically increase in the future. In fact, most recent studies show that from 2008 to 2010, the number of Asian-Americans marrying outside of their race dipped by 10 percent to 28 percent. It seems the trend among Asian-Americans nowadays is to marry other Asians.[52] No one knows what will happen to the American demographic in the next two generations, but there seems to be no scientific scholarly study that can overturn the projections of the Census Bureau and the marriage trends seem to be leaning toward marriage within the same race for Asians in general and within the same ethnicity at least for the Koreans in Los Angeles County.

One critical piece of information on Asian-American intermarriage is that the majority of intermarrying at the present is done by Asian females.[53]

---

[51] Harvie M. Conn, *The American City and the Evangelical Church: A Historical Overview* (Baker 1994), 130-131. The exact figure is obtained from the US Census Bureau. See www.census.gov/popluaton/projectioins/nation/nprh3550.txt (accessed May 15, 1999). According to Pew Research Center's projections in 2008, the US population in 2050 will be 439 million. Of these whites will be 47%, Hispanics 29%, blacks 13% and Asians 9%.
See http://www.pewhispanic.org/2008/02/11/us-population-projections- 2005-2050/ (accessed January 15, 2014).
[52] See http://www.pewsocialtrends.org/topics/intermarriage/ (accessed January 15, 2014).
[53] There are many suggested reasons for this phenomenon. First, Asian females are more readily accepted by white males. Second,

In 1984, again in Los Angeles County, out of 543 couples with at least one Korean partner who were married, 47 were intermarriages. Among them 78.6 percent were Korean females marrying non-Koreans. From personal observations, often times, unless the Asian female is very ethnic-conscious, most will follow their husbands to white churches or multiethnic churches. Asian males, however, usually marry other Asians. Even if they marry non-Asians, they tend to attend churches that are of their ethnic background This is so because Asian males seem to have a harder time assimilating into the white male-dominated society than their female counterparts—possibly due to white male's perception of the Asian male as too distant ethnically. One clear indicator of the racial barrier that exists between Korean immigrants and their offspring, and more particularly the male Koreans and whites, is what Emory Bogardus describes as the "distance" that white Americans in general feel toward other ethnic groups:

---

females tend to assimilate better than males. Third, there aren't that many Asian males who are socio-economically more upwardly mobile than Asian females for females tend to marry men who are socio-economically better. Fourth, the American media's portrayal of the Asian male has been degrading and distorted. In other words, almost all attractive male lead roles on TV and movies are mostly white males. As a result, many Asian women seem to be conditioned by the media to perceive Asian males as less than desirable. See Stanley Sue and James K. Morishima, The Mental Health of Asian Americans: Contemporary Issues in Identifying and Treating Mental Problems (Jossey-Bass, 1982), 105-116. According to Pew Research Center, in 2008, 50.8% of American-born Asian women marry outside of their race while about 20% of Asian-American men did the same. See http://pewsocialtrends.org/files/2010/10/755-marrying- out. pdf (accessed January 15, 2014).

Over a period of several decades, in the Bogardus "racial distance scale" Koreans have consistently ranked as one of the most "distant" racial ethnic groups by the white dominant group, and on one occasion were perceived by whites as the most distant racially.[54]

Of course, Koreans and other Asians have progressed in the mainstream society in many ways. But it seems that much Asian progress has been from white "acceptance" of Asian females. Most Asian males, therefore, tend to yearn for a more comfortable home where they can have dignity and not be treated as second-class members.[55]

If this pattern holds, it is my personal projection that in the future Asian-American churches will consist primarily of Asian males and their wives (both ethnic and non-ethnic) and a smaller number of strongly ethnic-conscious Asian females and their willing non-Asian husbands.

A Solution: Oikos Principle

---

[54] Milton J. Coalter, John M. Mulder and Louis B. Weeks, eds. *The Diversity of Discipleship: Presbyterians and Twentieth-Century Christian Witness* (Westminster/John Knox Press, 1991), 315.

[55] As with most husband/wife situations, it is observed in church situations that wives (usually Asians) of Korean men are more willing to follow the husbands when it comes to choosing a church. The only exception would be when the Asian wife of a non-Asian who is foreign born or less Americanized or not fluent in English. In this case, the wife prefers an Asian church and the non-Asian husband usually yields.

We've been talking about ethnically homogeneous ministries so far, but homogeneity can be cut in many different ways. A church might be thoroughly multiethnic on the outside, but when one analyzes other aspects of the congregation such as economic status, education, career and age, it might be as homogenous as an ethnically monolithic church. For example, a church that has 10 percent each of ten different ethnic groups still might be homogeneous in other areas. They actually might be upper middle class, college educated Yuppies in their 20's and 30's.

A good example of this is Newsong Community Church in Irvine, California. The church prides itself as intentionally multiethnic, but the largest ethnic group within the church, especially its leadership, is still Korean.[56] They claim that there is a certain degree of ethnic diversity in the congregation, but the overwhelming majority of the members are still Asian. In effect, instead of multiethnic they should be called

---

[56] Newsong Community Church's average age of members is 28. About 15% are college age and 65% single. About 35% are Chinese, 35% are Korean 10% are other Asian, 17% Caucasian and 3% African American and Latino. See Tini Tran, "Pan-Asian Churches Emerging." *Los Angeles Times*, March 8, 1999, Column One. Ten years later in 2009, Newsong's diversity remains about the same with 38.6% Chinese, 37.2% Korean, 9.9% other Asia-Pacific, and 3.7% African-American and Latino. Singles accounted for 56.3% and married 42.3%. It is interesting to note that despite the fact that there are four times as many Korean churches as Chinese churches in the US, at Newsong and other Asian –American churches, more Chinese seem to be present than Koreans. This might be due to the fact that Koreans have a lot more options in terms of available English ministries than the Chinese.

biethnic, for most of the members are either Korean or Chinese.[57] From another perspective, the church is very homogeneous. It caters to young adults who are English-speaking Asians, highly educated, and from middle to upper middle class in the socio-economic spectrum.

However, ethnicity is one of the most controversial issues facing the church today, and we must address it biblically and courageously. We must face the question: Is intentionally promoting a homogenous ministry biblical? We know that the Bible allows gentiles to be Christians in a gentile way and Jews in a Jewish way. We should conclude that Asians must be encouraged to practice their faith in an Asian way. What is true in the mission field is also true in ethnic ministries. One must contextualize the gospel so that people would be able to understand it better and furthermore encourage the people to theologize the gospel themselves so that they would be free to become who they are in Christ instead of being forced to conform to the image of the dominant group. This will, in turn, promote God-given ethnic dignity.

---

[57] There is a good reason why most Asian pastor-led multiethnic churches are biethnic, with Korean dominating the leadership, if not membership. The majority of Asian Christians in the US are Korean (about 4000 churches out of 7,000). Next is the Chinese church with about 1,200 churches. Japanese and other Asian Christians are a very small minority in the Asian-American Christian community. So, it is obvious that multiethnic Asian churches are mostly Korean and Chinese with Koreans often dominating the pastoral staff and membership due to a flood of Korean seminary graduates in the US. See http://l2foundation.org/2009/how-many-asian-american-churches-in-the-usa (accessed January 16, 2014).

Even as we accept and encourage ethnic diversity in the church catholic, however, we must not forget the church is first Christian, then ethnic. As Wagner puts it, "the homogeneous church must be inclusive, free to choose its path and exhibit community in a special and specific way."[58] A church that is not inclusive either ethnically or socio-economically or generationally or even linguistically is a church on its way to apostasy. In this sense, the Apartheid church in South in South Africa and the segregated Southern churches were apostate churches. As Dr. Sang Hyun Lee succinctly puts it:

> To forget our Asian past is sin. To despise it is rebellion against, or unfaithfulness to, the God of all histories and all times…Ethnicity is a gift of God, but is not God himself. That is why ultra nationalistic separatist absorption in our own ethnic enclaves is an act of idolatry.[59]

So, instead of the homogeneous unit principle which has too much focus on ethnic uniformity, *oikos principle* is proposed in its place. The end result may be similar to homogeneous unit principle, but instead of ethnic uniformity as its focus, providing home (*oikos* in Greek) is the emphasis in this paradigm. Instead of intentionally advocating a homogeneous or a heterogeneous church, the church should and must take everything possible to make its people feel at home. This approach starts with the local church from where

---

[58] C. Peter Wagner, *Our Kind of People: The Ethnic Dimensions of Church Growth in America* (John Knox Press, 1979), 158.
[59] Sang Hyun Lee and John V. Moore, eds. *Korean American Ministry* (PCUSA, 1993), 51-52.

43

they are, instead of artificially or forcibly integrating or segregating. This approach does not criticize or perpetually promote ethnically and socio-economically homogeneous or multiethnic churches. Oikos Principle recognizes that many minorities look at ethno-cultural relevance first when selecting a church but that's not all that draws people. Some are attracted because of doctrine, worship style, preaching, fellowship or other factors. Whatever the reason, the church must provide a home for them. Everyone must be encouraged to come and, at the same time, a home focus must be maintained.

The First Epistle of Peter's teaching on the home or house (*oikos*) of God's people is but one of numerous passages and teachings concerning the home motif in both the Old Testament and the New Testament. Peter addresses the believers in Asia as stranger or "paroikos" in the world. The Greek word is a composite word which has two parts "par" and "oikos." It denotes people who are homeless, dwelling in another's house. John Elliott describes them as strangers and aliens:

> In this general sense *paroikoi* are strangers, foreigners, aliens, people who are not at home, or who lack native roots, in the language, customs, culture, or political, social, and religious allegiances of the people among whom they dwell.[60]

---

[60] John H. Elliott, *A Home for the Homeless* (Fortress Press, 1981), 24.

The First Epistle of Peter does not stop at calling the believers "homeless" but instructs them that they have a new home. This new home is called "a spiritual house" (2:5) and "family or house of God" (4:17). As Elliott puts in succinctly:

> *Oikos* is my house and home with all its personnel and property, my family and lineage, my "given identity", the place where I "belong" and exercise my personal and communal rights and responsibilities, my moral obligations. The verb *oikein* means "to inhabit, permanently reside, to be at home." The adjective *oikeios* denotes domestic affairs, kinship bonds, and that which is personal, private, or proper to oneself…these and many related *oik-* terms refer to kith and kin, friend and brother, the familiar and the familial…*oikos* connotes associations and impressions of home, belongingness, and one's proper place…[61]

Furthermore, Elliott contends that the promise of home is not only in the eschatological future but here and now. In other words, God has given the socially homeless or estranged Christians the church as a new family or a new home in the temporal world.

> The addressees of I Peter were *paroikoi* by virtue of their social condition, not by virtue of their "heavenly home." The alternative to this marginal social condition of which I Peter

---

[61] Ibid., 24.

speaks is not an ephemeral "heaven is our home" form of consolation but the new home and social family to which the Christians belong here and now; namely, the *oikos tou theou*.[62]

The home or house motif runs throughout the Bible. The home is what God offers to the redeemed people of God. From the house of Israel where God's people functioned as an extended family to the house churches in the New Testament, God's people were given identity, family and community to be nurtured and loved by their new fathers, mothers, sisters and brothers.

Letty M. Russell, in her book *Household of Freedom* encourages theologians to use the power of the biblical metaphors to help people understand how they can order their own social and personal relationships.

> A metaphor, on the other hand, is an imaginative way of describing what is still unknown by using an example from present concrete reality. To say "I live in the 'Master's house'" is to provide a metaphorical description of one's position of subordination…To say "I live in a household of freedom" is to use a metaphorical description of one's freedom to participate with others in a community of mutual caring, drawn from the concrete experience of the

---

[62] John H. Elliott, *A Home for the Homeless* (Fortress Press, 1981), 130.

slaves living in Pharaoh's "house of bondage" and then moving out as the people of God toward a new "house of freedom."[63]

Many estranged English-speaking ethnics are strangers, foreigners or transient visitors who are socially separated, culturally alienated and personally deprived in the American society. They are in need of a home and many are still searching a church that they feel at home. Indeed, many English-speaking Asians are homeless even within the mainstream American church in general and their respective ethnic churches in America in particular. English-speaking Asians need not just any house or home but a household of freedom: a house of freedom in which those who dwell in it can find a way to nurture life without paying the price of being locked into roles of permanent domination and subordination.[64] Many Asians are doubly estranged from the mother church as well as the mainstream church. They need a home where they are free to drop artificial Anglo American norms or narrow ethnic cultural conformity and to creatively become who they are as a better expression of Christ-given call to be both Asian and American Christians. This liberation from the bondage of cultural tyranny from both the mother and host cultures will give them freedom to explore the possibility of creative potential. For many English-speaking Asian-Americans, the only home to be free is the English-speaking ethnic or Asian church. They must be given a home promised by God. So as

---

[63] Letty M. Russell, *Household of Freedom: Authority in Feminist Theology* (The Westminster Press, 1987), 37.
[64] Ibid., 41.

Ephesians 2:19 declares "you are no longer foreigners and aliens, but fellow citizens with God's people and members of God's household...", they can finally come home and feel safe in a haven of rest.

This is true of all who seek a spiritual home. Whether they be nuclear ethnics (immigrants requiring non-English churches) or marginal ethnics (bilingual churches or ethnic English ministries), alienated ethnics (at home in Anglo churches) or cross-cultural ethnics (multiethnic churches), Jesus invites us to his Father's home:

> Do not let your hearts be troubled. Trust in God; trust also in me. In my Father's house are many rooms; if it were not so, I would have told you. I am going there to prepare a place for you. And if I go and prepare a place for you, I will come back and take you to be with me that you also may be where I am. (John 14:1-3)

In the Father's house, there are many rooms where different groups within the Kingdom of God could finally find a place to call home.

Many English-speaking Asians are neither at home in all-white or ethnic churches. The home for them is an English-language ministry which has a unique culture of its own (neither exclusively American or Asian but a third culture), one that they can identify with and at the same time that is inclusive so that the members of different ethnic backgrounds still will feel welcomed. This is a church that is both ethnic and multiethnic. Can it be done? I believe so. Jesus was fully human and fully divine. As followers of Christ, we should all strive to be more like Jesus.

section two

the project

chapter three

a case study:
an english-speaking congregation

A Brief History

The Korean Presbyterian Church was founded in 1973 in Vienna, Virginia.[65] About a year later, it was renamed the Korean Central Presbyterian Church (KCPC), which it remains today.[66] Rev. Won Sang Lee, was called and installed in 1977.[67] On June 6, 1985, the congregation voted to affiliate with the Presbyterian Church in America (PCA) denomination.

The church has grown steadily since its founding and in 1999, had an average weekly attendance exceeding 2,000.[68] It is one of the largest churches among the 220 Korean churches in the PCA and is regarded as one of the most influential churches in the

---

[65] 1999 Directory of the Korean Central Presbyterian Church., 6. KCPC is presently located in Centreville, VA.

[66] The Korean version of the church name is transliterated as "Washington Central Presbyterian Church". The reason why it's rendered "Korean Central Presbyterian Church" is to make it easier for Koreans to find the church in phone directories, newspapers and other publications. Since the Korean language version of the church name is always written in Korean, the name "Korean" was not necessary.

[67] Since writing of this report, Rev. Lee has retired from the pastorate and serves as Pastor Emeritus to this day.

[68] As of 2014, KCPC has about 4,500 worshipers on a given Sunday.

nation. [69] KCPC's English-speaking congregation is likewise regarded highly, and is considered an innovative and advanced English-language church model for ethnic Koreans in North America.

KCPC began providing an English-language service in 1986, to serve the increasing numbers of adult children of the Korean-speaking members as well as other English-speaking adults who were attending the church. As time passed, however, it became clear to church leaders that an English service alone wasn't enough to minister effectively to English-speaking members, because of linguistic, cultural and generational differences. The church leaders concluded that the English-speaking congregation must be self-supporting, self-governing, and self-propagating to maintain its membership and reach out effectively to others who desired a similar culturally relevant ministry. [70]

Thus in 1992, an English-speaking congregation was formed within the mother church. It was granted broad authority to conduct its own ministry, including

---

[69] KCPC was selected as one of thirteen churches identified as a "good-to-great church" in the US. The study, conducted by the Southern Baptist Theological Seminary, examined 52,333 churches. The results were published in *Breakout Churches* by Thom S. Rainer (Zondervan Publishing Co., 2005). Another PCA church, Sarang Community Church of Anaheim, CA is the largest Korean church in the PCA. In fact, Sarang is the largest Asian church in North America with about 10,000 worshipers as of 2014.

[70] The Nevius Principle, which was the core evangelistic philosophy used by the missionaries to the Far East in the last two centuries, helped the churches in the mission field to explode in growth and strength, as can be seen most clearly in the Korean church.

the ability to accept new members on its own and administration of the sacraments by the English ministry pastor. With the exception of full financial independence and its own board of elders, the English-speaking congregation was functioning effectively as a separate church.[71]

According to the church directory, even though there had been many pastors who ministered to the congregation on a part-time basis, the first recognized, full-time pastor of the English-speaking congregation was Pastor D, who was called and installed in 1990. Under his leadership, the congregation's weekly average attendance grew to about 100. [72] After ministering less than a year in the pastorate, however, Pastor D resigned to plant an independent English-speaking church in the Chicago area.[73]

In 1993, Pastor R, a single in mid-twenties, was called as the second full-time pastor of the English-speaking congregation. Subsequently, ordained in the Evangelical Free church, Pastor R was the first KCPC pastor to speak only English at the church. From the beginning, language, cultural, generational, and age barriers resulted in much conflict between Pastor R and the Korean-speaking leaders as well as the (mostly married) English-speaking leaders.[74]

---

[71] This information was gathered through direct contact with pastors, elders and members of the church.

[72] This figure is based on attendance records in the weekly worship bulletins of the English language service.

[73] Pastor D subsequently was called by KCPC as its senior pastor of the Korean congregation in 2003, who served there until 2012 when again he was called by Sarang Community Church as senior pastor.

[74] This information is based on interviews with some of the key leaders of the English-speaking congregation.

Nevertheless, under his leadership, the congregation almost doubled its weekly average attendance and was granted financial autonomy from the mother church.[75]

Pastor R's tenure with the church came to an end following tensions over the drafting of a vision statement for the English-speaking congregation. Originally intended to unite the congregation with a common purpose and direction for the future, the vision statement ended up exacerbating the differences among the congregation members.

The initial proposed vision statement was overtly ethnocentric, to the dismay of Pastor R and some of the

---

[75] An interesting pattern in the membership growth of English-speaking congregations is that it is often concurrent with the growth spurts in their Korean-speaking congregations. KCPC English-speaking congregation's weekly attendance plateau of about 230 since 1995 corresponds to the Korean-speaking congregation's plateau of about 2,000 over the same period. All the Korean-American English-speaking congregations in North America personally known to the author show the same growth relationship between the mother and daughter churches. The Korean-speaking/English-speaking membership ratio seems to be about 10:1. Only the independent Korean-American English-speaking churches show growth directly related to the ministry ability of their pastors and other church leaders. For example, an independent Asian-American church in Irvine, CA, Newsong Community Church, has weekly average attendance of over 700 only after four years in existence. See Tini Tran, "Pan-Asian Churches Emerging," *Los Angeles Times*, March 8, 1999, Column One. Newsong subsequently mushroomed quickly to about 5,000 in the 2000s and now has stabilized to about 2,000 as of 2014. Another independent Korean-American campus church called "Covenant Fellowship Church" in Urbana–Champaign, Illinois has about 600 attendees.
See www.cfchome.org/about_us/demographics (accessed May 5, 1999).

single English-speaking Korean-Americans within the congregation.[76] Their efforts to alter it did not succeed, as several of the (mostly married) lay leaders of the congregation opposed the pastor's preferred explicitly multiethnic vision for the church.

As Pastor R was unable to follow his multiethnic vision for KCPC English Congregation, and for other reasons, he resigned in June 1996, and planted an independent, multiethnic church in March 1997 in Northern Virginia near KCPC. Some of the singles who shared the vision joined him.[77]

Before his departure, Pastor R recommended that the congregation invite his friend, Pastor J, to serve as KCPC's third English ministry pastor. In another major step towards governance autonomy, the English-speaking congregation selected the new pastor themselves, voting for the first time in a congregational meeting.

From the beginning of his ministry in August 1996, the new pastor seemed to connect better with both congregations. This was probably due to the fact that

---

[76] This information was gathered from an interview with a long-time leader of the English-speaking congregation. The adopted vision statement of the English-speaking congregation was "To reach out to and equip those in the Washington DC metropolitan area who identify with the Korean-American culture through reverent worship, biblical teaching and small group discipleship in an affirming family atmosphere to be Christ's ambassadors to the world."

[77] As of 1999, Pastor R's church is about 100. They are mostly singles and English-speaking Koreans plus a handful of English-speaking Chinese who came out of a local Chinese church with their English-speaking Chinese pastor who joined Pastor R as an assistant pastor. In 2000, Pastor R moved back to California to plant another church in the Orange County area.

Pastor J could speak Korean, was married and had children—to the delight both of the English-speaking congregation leadership and the married couples of the English-speaking congregation, who make up more than half of the English-speaking membership.

Another reason the new pastor connected better was that he was the English-speaking congregation's first PCA minister. [78] Pastor R's non-Presbyterian affiliation had been the major cause of his inability to take the congregation independent. (His wish that they join the Evangelical Free Church was vetoed by the elders of the mother church.)[79]

As a member of an Anglo presbytery in the PCA, Pastor J was better positioned to assist the English congregation in their transition from a dependent congregation of a church in the Korean-language presbytery to independence in the local Anglo presbytery.[80]

This step was critical to the planned autonomy of the English-speaking congregation because few of its

---

[78] Because of the scarcity of English-speaking pastors, pastors from non-PCA denominations were called by KCPC prior to calling the present pastor.

[79] His desire to take the congregation into the Evangelical Free Church was relayed to the author by Pastor R over the phone in 1993 shortly after his arrival at KCPC.

[80] Of its seventy-five presbyteries, PCA also has eight Korean-language presbyteries. This situation is extremely beneficial for the Korean churches in the denomination because the mother churches and daughter churches can remain in the same location and denomination while belonging to different language presbyteries. Anglo denomination without Korean language presbyteries will have a harder time recruiting Korean churches and Korean-American denominations without English language presbyteries will not be able to retain English-speaking pastors and churches.

members could speak Korean well and many members were not even ethnically Korean. If the daughter congregation failed to join an Anglo presbytery, the church would not be able to fully participate in the life of the presbytery because of the language barrier. Also, the church would have a greater difficulty finding and ordaining pastors willing and able to function in a Korean-language presbytery.

As of this writing, despite the advantages mentioned above, the English-speaking congregation has not made a final decision to join the Anglo presbytery.[81] This is primarily due to the reluctance of the mother church to give the final go ahead, due in part to a fear of the daughter becoming disconnected in its independence. Church elders remember clearly how many English congregation members left with Pastor R and see that, though the exits are down in number, they still haven't ceased. The elders may fear another such situation in the future.

Should this happen, it would be detrimental to the mother church. One reason is that most of the teachers for the children and youth ministries come from the English-speaking congregation. Without them, the education ministry would be handicapped in many ways.

But such fears may be misplaced. Both congregations are committed to staying together even

---

[81] In 2006, KCPC English Ministry was renamed Christ Central Presbyterian Church upon joining the Korean Capital Presbytery (PCA) as a mission church. In 2010, CCPC moved to a new facility in Centreville with its own worship center within the bigger church complex. Finally, in 2011, CCPC ordained its first ruling elder to form a session with the organizing pastor, thus becoming an independent church alongside the mother church.

after the full autonomy, and both are committed to drafting a covenant to that effect.[82]

The Congregation

Korean Central Presbyterian Church is located in affluent Fairfax County in Northern Virginia near Washington DC. Due to its proximity to the nation's capital, the county has become a showcase of America's ever-increasing cultural and ethnic diversity. According to its local government, by the year 2000, Fairfax County's total population reached near 970,000. By 2020, the population is projected to reach 1,160,000.[83] According to 1996 figures, the ethnic distribution of Fairfax County is 68 percent white, 12.4 percent Asian, 8.4 percent Hispanic, and 8.3 percent black.[84] The residents are highly educated and affluent compared to the rest of the state and the nation as a whole.[85]

---

[82] This commitment to stay together was confirmed from many personal conversations between the two senior pastors of the two language congregations and their leaders.

[83] The figures were obtained from the website: http://www.fairfaxcounty.gov/demogrph (accessed January 9, 2014) and are rounded here for greater statistical significance than in the original.

[84] See http://www.fairfaxcounty.gov/demogrph (accessed January 9, 2014). By 2012, Fairfax County's ethnic makeup has changed to 62.8% white, 18% Asian, 16.1% Hispanic, and 9% black.

[85] According to 1996 figure, 56.3% of residents 25 years and older were college graduates compared to 23.6% for the national average. At $70,000, Fairfax County's 1995 median household income is twice that of either Virginia or the United States. See http://www.fairfaxcounty.gov/demogrph (accessed January 9, 2014). In 2012, 58.3% of the residents of the same age group were

The congregation matches the county statistics in economic and educational achievement. Almost all are college graduates and many have master's or doctorate degrees. However, the congregational ethnic makeup is predominantly English-speaking Korean. They are mostly children of the immigrants who arrived after 1965 when the Chinese Exclusion Act was lifted after over 80 years of effective screening out of most would-be Asian immigrants. As a result, almost all of the English-speaking Koreans are between ages of 18 and 35 at the time of the survey.[86] The majority was born in Korea, but due to their young ages at the time of immigration, their proficiency in the mother tongues is less than conversational. About 10 percent of the congregation is non-Korean. However, they almost always have a Korean connection. They are married to a Korean or have adopted Korean children or have Korean friends or are attracted to Koreans and their culture.

There are three major age or life-stage groups in the congregation: college, young singles and couples. The first is the college-age group. Most of them are the children of the Korean-speaking congregation. Almost all of them grew up in KCPC and joined the English-speaking congregation upon graduation from high school. Although there are about 100 of their names listed in the English-congregation's directory, most are out-of-town college students. The only time they regularly attend their home church is during the summer (if they stay home at all). Every year about 15

---

college graduates and the median household income was over $107,000.

[86] This data is from church membership data.

to 20 graduate from college, but very few return to their home church because they continue to graduate school or find jobs far away. Resident college students are less than 20 in number and college-age members not attending college are virtually zero. They seem to feel out of place in a highly educated English-speaking congregation.

Singles make up roughly half of the resident members of the congregation. There are about 100 singles, most of whom are in their 20's. Almost all are college graduates and professionals. This group is the most transient of the three major age groups represented in the congregation due to frequent job transfers, marriage or graduate school enrollments. Some of them grew up in KCPC but the overwhelming majority is from out-of-town.

Over half of the members in the English-speaking congregation are married and many of them have children. In 1999, there were about 65 couples, with about 70 children in all. Nearly all of the couples are in their 30s. Some attend KCPC with their parents, but most do not have parents who are members of the Korean-speaking congregation. Married couples contribute the most to congregational stability by long-term membership and providing most of the leadership and financial support. All of the ordained deacons are married and married couples give most of the weekly offering of about $6,000.

The Vision Statement Controversy

Ever since the English worship started at KCPC, there have always been a small number of non-Koreans attending the service. The English-speaking congregation has always tried to embrace them and seems to have been very sensitive to their needs to feel at home. However, during the pastorate of Pastor R, the issue of ethnicity surfaced and deeply divided the church. During a process of drafting a vision statement for the English-speaking congregation, two opposing views came into direct conflict.

One view, espoused by the pastor and a small number of single English-speaking Koreans, mandated that the church rid itself of the ethnocentric phrase in the proposed vision statement, which said the church is to reach out to and equip those "who identify with the Korean-American culture." According to their view of Scripture, Christian ministry must transcend culture and ethnicity. They believed it is unbiblical to focus on a particular ethnic group while other ethnic groups in the community also need to hear the gospel and be welcomed into a nearby church. While acknowledging that the church will always attract more Koreans because of its ties to the mother church and the Korean-American pastor, they felt that a blunt statement favoring one ethnic group was contrary to the scriptural teaching of the unity of all believers in Christ.

Those who wanted to make the ministry a special ethnic ministry focused on reaching out to and nurturing English-speaking Korean-Americans defended the statement as it was. They noted that there are thousands of predominantly white churches and hundreds of black churches in the DC area but only a handful of English-language Korean-American churches. If this handful loses its focus to become multiethnic, those English-speaking Korean-Americans who need a culturally specific ministry would be deprived of a home. While whites and blacks will probably always have their churches, they argued, Koreans will lose theirs if forced to become multiethnic. This would be detrimental not only to many members but also to outreach efforts to unchurched English-speaking Koreans. Besides, they argued, the phrase "who identify with the Korean-American culture" is broad enough to embrace all who want to be a part of KCPC since they will in some way "identify with the Korean-American culture.

After much debate, the vision statement was adopted with the ethnic-specific language through the support of the Korean-speaking congregation and the majority of the English-speaking congregation. His vision not shared by the majority of the congregation, Pastor R ultimately decided to plant a church that would strive to become a deliberately multiethnic congregation.[87]

The vote and Pastor J's arrival notwithstanding, KCPC has had a number of skirmishes and conflicts because of the vision statement. During the congregation's singles retreat in 1997, the Korean-American guest speaker who had been born and raised in the US and who once was a proponent of assimilation, criticized those who wanted Korean churches to become multiethnic as untenable and biblically wrong. Several singles and, more particularly, one non-Korean woman and her Korean-American boyfriend, took offense and complained that the messages were too ethnocentric. Unhappy, the couple

---

[87] Pastor R's church within a couple of years reached over a hundred regular worshippers with Koreans as still the dominant group.

eventually left the church; and even those who remained have expressed discomfort since the retreat.

A second incident occurred in the summer of 1998, when three members associated with a parachurch organization in the area left the church, taking with them a small number of recent college graduates who grew up in the church. One of the reasons expressed for leaving was their discomfort with the Korean-American ministry focus, which they felt hindered their efforts to reach out to other Asians, including, for example, local Vietnamese.

The above incidents sparked yet another look at the vision statement, this time in the broader context of long-term planning. The focus of debate was the Advisory Board, which reflected the divisions of the past. Once again, one party wanted to delete the phrase "who identify with the Korean-American culture" from the vision statement while one prominent member of the Advisory Board adamantly rejected any idea of revision.

After repeated meetings and prayer gatherings among the English-speaking congregation's Advisory Board members and consultation with the Korean-speaking congregation's session, a compromise was reached. While agreeing to delete the controversial phrase, a brief history of the English-speaking congregation was included as an addendum to the statement explaining the original purpose of the Korean-speaking congregation in establishing the English-speaking congregation.[88]

---

[88] The brief description of the history of the English-speaking congregation stated that the Korean-speaking congregation started the English-language ministry to spiritually nurture the English-speaking adult children and to reach out to the English-speaking

While the debate over the vision statement went on, the name of the church was another source of debate and discomfort among some of the members. A small number of parishioners expressed their concern over the word "Korean" in the official name of the church and indicated that the name does not reflect accurately the current membership of the English-speaking congregation. They argued that an ethnic-specific name, while appropriate for the Korean-speaking mother congregation, was inappropriate for the English-speaking daughter congregation, because it gave non-Koreans and Koreans alike an impression that non-Koreans are not welcome in the church. Some acknowledged that even though the name change would not drastically alter the composition of the church, it would, nevertheless, make non-Korean members feel more at home at KCPC and be less of a hindrance both to Koreans who feel uncomfortable with the ethnocentric name and to non-Koreans who feel like strangers in a predominantly Korean-American congregation.[89]

However, many members, including non-Koreans, felt the original church name should be kept because of its high name recognition. KCPC is so well known in the area and all over the United States within the Korean community that if the English-speaking

---

Korean-Americans in the area who need a culturally relevant ministry.

[89] According to the final project survey, 70% of the respondents expressed comfort with the church name. Of the 30% who felt uncomfortable, 90% of them were English-speaking Koreans. Seventy percent of all non-Korean respondents expressed comfort with the church name. See Appendix One #21 and Appendix Two #21.

congregation adopted another name, it was feared that its outreach potential would seriously be compromised. According to some, it would be like "Taco Bell" wanting to change its name to "Mexican Bell" because franchise desires the customers to know that it does not sell only tacos. With such a change, the restaurant would probably suffer much due to lost name recognition.

Moreover, they argued, English-speaking Korean-Americans who want to attend an English-language Korean church also need to look up the name "Korean" to find one. Whether one is Korean-speaking or English-speaking, a descriptive name of the church makes it easier to find the church through newspapers, the *Yellow Pages*, or even the Internet.

No leadership move was made to change the church's name and after some debate among the members, the discussion faded away. Given the history of the church, however, it's likely that the issue will resurface in the near future.[90]

From the very beginning, the vision statement controversy has been an outward manifestation of the two schools of thought both theologically and sociologically at odds in the congregation. Theologically, there are those who emphasize the catholicity and unity of the church on one hand and, on the other, those who espouse contextualization of the gospel in the local church level to make it relevant for the people. Sociologically, there are idealists who

---

[90] Since the writing of this report in 1999, Korean Central Presbyterian Church (KCPC) English-speaking Congregation has changed its name to Christ Central Presbyterian Church in 2005, joining the mother church's Korean Capital Presbytery (PCA) as a mission church.

desire cultural and ethnic pluralism in the church (which seems to be the trend of the rest of the American society) and pragmatists who want culturally safe and ethnically comfortable environments within the church (that churches which are more or less homogenous grow the best). What seems to usually end up happening is extreme application of the two views, producing two radically different results: Anglo-conformist multiethnic church or Judaizing ethnocentric church.[91]

---

[91] What usually ends up happening when a church declares itself multiethnic is that instead of becoming multicultural church, it becomes another ethno-cultural church that espouses Anglo culture in which everyone speaks and behaves like whites. On the other hand, when a church becomes very ethnocentric, it ceases to be truly Christian church and follows the path of the ethnocentric heretics called the Judaizers of the early church who required gentiles to become Jewish before becoming Christian.

chapter four

the research

The Working Theory

This project was undertaken to study English-speaking Koreans in a Korean-American church.[92] Because of the debate in the Korean-American church on whether an ethnic English-speaking ministry is needed in a multiethnic and multicultural society like America, the people who attend such a ministry (Korean Central Presbyterian Church in Virginia) were studied. The question under consideration is: "Do English-speaking Koreans need an English-language ethnic ministry?"

To understand this better, a working theory, "Most English-speaking Korean-American church-goers look at ethnicity first when selecting a church" was tested on the members of this particular congregation. Through a survey, the project attempts to answer whether the English-speaking Koreans attend this particular ethnic church because it's Korean-American or for some other reason.

---

[92] The project was guided by a handbook on D.Min. projects. See Richard E. Davies, *Handbook for Doctor of Ministry Projects: An Approach to Structured Observation of Ministry* (University Press, 1984).

Focus Groups

The approval to implement the final project having been given and two faculty advisors having been assigned by the Doctor of Ministry Studies Committee at Princeton Theological Seminary, two representative focus groups were convened to elicit from the congregation a variety of thoughts, feelings and positions at work in the issue of ethnicity and ethnic churches so that a well-crafted survey could be drafted for the whole congregation.[93]

A moderator and a note-taker were assigned to each group. Prior to the discussions, they were briefly explained the purpose of the focus group. The group discussion—each an hour and a half—were taped for later analysis with the notes. After each discussion, the note-taker summarized the discussion for thirty minutes to make sure every major item was correctly understood by all and accurately recorded. Following each focus group meeting, the group leaders were debriefed to review the most important themes or ideas expressed, the most noteworthy quotes, and any unexpected or unanticipated findings. Finally, the focus group questions and discussion methods were evaluated to see how they required further revisions or adjustments.

Ten focus group questions were culled from lists submitted by the moderators. For purposes of continuity and consistency, these questions were

---

[93] Richard A. Krueger, *Focus Groups: A Practical Guide for Applied Research* (Sage, 1994). This book was used as basis for planning, drafting questionnaire, recruiting participants and conducting focus groups.

included in the final survey along with other questions formulated from the focus group discussions.

Focus Group One (Ethnics)

This focus group was intentionally made up only of English-speaking Koreans so they could speak freely without being too conscious of non-Koreans. The participants were carefully chosen to represent the congregation accurately and reflect various opinions there. Thus, four of the seven were married and three were singles. Three were bilingual and four were more or less monolingual. Four were men and three women. Following are brief reports of the discussion for each of the ten questions.

1. What do you think most English-speaking Korean-Americans first look at in a church when deciding on one?

From the outset it was obvious this group of all English-speaking Korean-Americans was very ethnocentric, even though about a half of them were American-born Koreans. All agreed that most English-speaking Koreans look at ethnicity first when choosing a church.

Typical comments by these participants included:

> Koreans in particular look for a Korean church...African-Americans too.

> Ethnicity first for Korean-Americans, since they live scattered; church brings the

community together, unlike the Chinese... who live in ethnic neighborhoods.

As Asians we have a natural affiliation to one another.

2. What kind of needs do you think the English-speaking Korean-Americans have at the present which would warrant a specialized ministry for them?

The answer was basically to provide a comfort zone. One of the participants indicated that culture is not probably the main reason for coming to a Korean-American church because most English-speaking Koreans are more American in culture than Korean. According to some being with people who look like them is the chief reason. The moderator and the note-taker expressed surprise during the debriefing that the reason this particular group of Korean-Americans attend a Korean-American church is not primarily because of culture but of Korean face, understanding this as an expression of racialism rather than cultural distinction.[94]

Typical comments by these participants included:

It's not ideology...we look different...I think more like white Christians.

---

[94] Racialism is different from racism in that it does not elevate one race above another. Nevertheless, race becomes an element that facilitates individual socialization in a variety of race-oriented comfort zones.

It's easier to share spiritual things with your own kind.

It gives us a sense of belonging...church is a place where we find that community.

Many people come to church for social reasons. There may be more non-Christians in an ethnic church...

3. What kind of church model do you envision for the ethnic churches in America?

    A. Melting Pot – All ethnic churches are integrated into one homogeneous church.
    B. Salad Bowl – Each church with a distinct approach contributes uniquely to the tapestry of a diverse American church.
    C. Stew – Each church retains its own characteristic but at the same time contributes to the church in general while itself is affected by others as well.

Another fascinating unanimous response from this particular group of Korean-Americans is that they all believe in the stew model of ethnic churches in America than the melting pot.

Typical comments by these participants included:

Stew model works [best] in missions... Korean churches [can most effectively] reach Koreans...and [so could] blacks and Hispanics...

Another way distinctively ethnic church can contribute uniquely to the American church in general is seen in how Koreans can [effectively] reach the Cherokees…better than whites.

4. What do you think Korean-American churches will look like in the future ethnically? How will they be different from now? How will they be the same?

Most could not envision an America without racially divided churches. Although many expect partial integration, full integration was regarded as neither possible nor desirable.

Typical comments by these participants included:

I don't envision it being 50/50. We'll see more integration through [inter]marriage… but not full integration.

Skin color matters both ways. I don't see that changing.

Initial racial filter isn't necessarily bad—unless that's dominant.

5. How and when does an ethnic church become multi-ethnic? How do you define multi-ethnic church?

The moderator decided to skip this question because of time.

6. Should an ethnic church with one dominant ethnic group try to allocate its resources evenly to reach out to all local ethnic groups even though the return is small or should it try to focus on a group that it is most effective in reaching?

Most agreed that having an outreach focus to Korean-Americans is logical and cost-effective.

Typical comments by these participants included:

If results are clearly better, focus is good.

Can't you do a little bit of both?

7. Who do you think feel most uncomfortable with the name "Korean" in KCPC among the English-speaking congregation member? Korean-Americans or non-Koreans?

On the issue of ethno-specific church name, most felt in the beginning of the discussion that non-Koreans would feel most uncomfortable with the name "Korean" in the church name. But later, some concluded that some Korean-Americans would feel uncomfortable with the name—especially if they tried to bring non-Korean friends to KCPC. Some indicated that ethno-specific names sometimes become problematic in evangelism, but nearly all participants felt that the name should stay.

Typical comments by these participants included:

Why do you ask this question? Why try to fix something that's not broken?

In some ways it's effective [to have ethno-specific name]—bringing in other Koreans. It's our niche.

I just realized I've never invited a non-Korean to come to church with me!

The name shouldn't hinder but it does.

8. Do you think non-Korean-American senior pastor of the English-speaking congregation would do an effective pastoral ministry?

This question caused the most heated discussion. Most did not think a non-Korean would be effective at KCPC because of lack of Korean cultural background. Many indicated that people wouldn't feel they could relate to non-Koreans.

Typical comments by these participants included:

No. He wouldn't have the same kind of background.

People wouldn't feel they could relate to non-Korean [pastors].

That's racist!

Maybe it is. But that's the way it is.

9. Is it important for you to raise your children in a Korean-American church? If yes, what are the most important personal reasons?

Many believed that parents, not the church, are responsible for instilling ethnic identity in children. Although instilling such identity is very important and participants said they'd prefer their children attend a Korean-American church, they said ultimately, it's their children's choice.

Typical comments by these participants included:

> No. Because it's parents' duty, not church's to instill ethnic identity.

> Yes, the ethnic identity is important.

> That's their [children's] business.

10. Should churches ever address ethno-cultural issues?

Finally, even though there was an overwhelming preference for an ethnic church, as far as cultural practices in the church are concerned, most participants felt that it's inappropriate to address ethno-cultural and ethno-political issues in the church. This is consistent with the survey results, which showed that while people do want ethno-culturally relevant ministry, they do not want the church to be too overtly ethnic in its ministry and practice.

Typical comments by these participants included:

Be sensitive to the issues but it shouldn't be the main focus of the church.

It shouldn't be church sanctioned.

This group's frank responses stunned both the moderator and the note-taker. They were expecting English-speaking Koreans to have cultural reasons for wanting to attend a Korean-American church but found instead that ethnic differences were more important than cultural. The leaders thought many of the comments were almost racist.

During the debriefing, many suggestions were made to clarify some of the questions and to facilitate the discussion. Most of these suggestions were implemented with the second focus group.

Focus Group Two (Mixed)

This group was multiethnic. Only three out of nine participants were English-speaking Koreans. The rest were: one Italian-American, one Japanese-American, one African-American, and three Anglo-Americans. These were mostly men, due to difficulty finding non-Korean females in the congregation. Most non-Koreans in the congregation are males married to Korean females. Of the nine participants, five were married. Among the three English-speaking Koreans only one was bilingual.

This group was chosen to find out what non-Koreans think about ethnic churches. As expected, even though three of the nine participants were English-speaking Koreans, most of the Koreans were very quiet and the non-Koreans dominated the discussion, with the exception of one bilingual woman who afterwards expressed her personal dismay at the direction of the discussion. The discussion and the opinions expressed in this particular multiethnic group were radically different from the first.

1. What do you think most English-speaking Korean-Americans first look at in a church when deciding on one?

When they were asked this, most could not answer the question except to say that comfort level is probably the most important factor in determining one's choice of church. The participants were then asked how they, themselves came to this particular Korean church. The non-Koreans who had adopted Korean children said that it was for their children's sake. One Caucasian man insisted, however, that the first thing that people look at was doctrine. Two single Caucasian men mentioned that they decided to come to the church because the members took a sincere interest in them and that the people were sincere in worshipping God.

Typical comments by these participants included:

> A sense of belonging…Do they fit into that church or culture or groups…Also, friendship between congregation members.

> When we first came here we were looking more for our daughter…looking to give her more of her heritage…We cannot impart to

her a sense of background that being around other Korean children could do.

We wanted to go to a Korean church so that our children could have that part of their culture.

For us, it was the religious doctrine issue.

I think a lot of people come to this church because their parents dragged them to this church...then they started an English ministry.

2. What kind of needs do you think the English-speaking Korean-Americans have at the present which would warrant a specialized ministry for them?

Some said it was the need to belong and still others mentioned outreach to Koreans both evangelistically and socio-politically. But the discussion soon led to assimilation. Some believed that the role of the Korean-American church is to help facilitate Koreans, particularly the immigrant generation, to be assimilated into the mainstream. One Korean-American threw herself into the discussion at the end to say the Korean-American church provides Korean-American Christian role model for Korean-American Christians.

Typical comments by these participants included:

Getting comfortable with American society ...makes them feel like they are a part of the society. To feel that their tradition in Korea is now our tradition here…to feel that their lives are a part of American society.

It's easier to get unreached people into an environment…to get to the doctrine.

It's needed to assimilate into [the mainstream] society.

It facilitates first generation into the second generation.

[Korean churches] seem to perpetuate a crutch…so people do not assimilate into the mainstream…[having Korean churches] is good and bad. I don't know how to rip them apart.

3. What kind of church model do you envision for the ethnic churches in America?

D. Melting Pot – All ethnic churches are integrated into one homogeneous church.
E. Salad Bowl – Each church with a distinct approach contributes uniquely to the tapestry of a diverse American church.
F. Stew – Each church retains its own characteristic but at the same time contributes to the church in general and itself is affected by others as well.

In their discussion about the future of the ethnic churches, the general consensus was that ideally churches should be a "melting pot" but this was unlikely to happen. Perhaps because of their expectation of what is realistic, this group chose "salad bowl" as the church model they envision for the ethnic churches in the US.

Typical comments by these participants included:

> I don't think you can have a church that is multiethnic. [However] I think that one church that has predominantly one ethnic group is a problem.

> Why would we want to have segregated churches? If we first try to be Christians, we should be comfortable going to any church.

> It's "stew". Churches are going to keep their own characteristics that will come into the "stew", but will not change what the "stew" is.

> I don't think a melting pot is possible because I don't think that this country is a melting pot.

4. What do you think Korean-American churches will look like in the future ethnically? How will they be different from now? How will they be the same?

This question was skipped by the moderator because of time limits.

5. How and when does an ethnic church become multi-ethnic? How do you define multi-ethnic church?

When asked how a church becomes multiethnic, one immediately mentioned a name change. Another suggested diverse membership. Still others stressed that the congregation must think of itself as multiethnic.

Typical comments by these participants included:

> How you change to a multiethnic church? You've got to change the name of the church.
>
> I think membership is critical…you must draw people in that are multiethnic.
>
> I would define our church as multi-racial because people are not really Korean in terms of daily culture…they are more American. I think that they are not as homogeneous, even though they look homogeneous.
>
> I think Koreans in the first generation are very ethnocentric. But younger people are more open. I would hope that people would want to worship with other ethnic groups since we are more open.

6. Should an ethnic church with one dominant ethnic group try to allocate its resources evenly to reach out to all local ethnic groups even though the return is small or should it try to focus on a group that it is most effective in reaching?

Most said that it all depends on what the mission of the church is, however, Christians must reach out to all ethnic groups to some degree.

Typical comments by these participants included:

> How good is it to allocate resources when
> there is no increase?

> We should just reach out to all people and not
> worry about different ethnic groups.

> Depends on the mission. If it is the church's
> mission than we should generalized [the
> resources] to other ethnic groups.

7. Who do you think feel most uncomfortable with the
name "Korean" in KCPC among the English-speaking
congregation member? Korean-Americans or non-
Koreans?

When asked whether Koreans or non-Koreans would
feel more uncomfortable with the name "Korean" in the
church name, generally the participants said both
groups could feel uncomfortable. It seemed on this
point they were evenly divided.

Typical comments by these participants included:

> I like it. I think that it would be an attraction.
> It's going to draw Koreans and not be a
> negative to non-Koreans.

> I think that churches that grow do not have the
> ethnic name.

8. Do you think non-Korean-American senior pastor of the English-speaking congregation would do an effective pastoral ministry?

Most said that a non-Korean pastor would conduct an effective pastoral ministry, but some newcomers may be disillusioned when they see a non-Korean pastor.

Typical comments by these participants included:

> In our ministry [a non-Korean senior pastor would be just as effective] because our ministry doesn't do outreach to Koreans.

> If the guy was a non-Korean, then a lot of newcomers will say, why is this church KCPC?

> If the English-speaking congregation was totally separate from the Korean-speaking congregation then yes, otherwise, no.

9. Is it important for you to raise your children in a Korean-American church? If yes, what are the most important personal reasons?

The moderator skipped this question.

10. Should churches ever address ethno-cultural issues?

When asked about the appropriateness of addressing Korean ethno-cultural issues in the church, the consensus was that churches should address them as long as it does not become a distraction from doing Christian ministry.

Typical comments by these participants included:

There should be Korean tradition.

A church's role is to provide cultural issues.

You have to have cultural elements. Otherwise, why have an ethnic church?

If these subjects can be brought up by doing it in a way to worship God.

In summary, the general consensus of this focus group is that there is a need for Korean ethnic churches for new immigrants. English-speaking ethnic churches are also needed as a bridge facilitating assimilation into the American culture. Having done so they should move toward becoming a truly multiethnic church.

Many in this particular group seemed to have had hard time understanding the issues involved in the Korean-American church. Basically, most participants in this group wanted the Korean church to move as quickly toward assimilation as possible. However, for the time being, they realized that there will be ethnic churches in America. Many of them wanted the church to reach out to all in the local community without focusing on the Koreans too much. However, since the church is an ethnic church at the moment, ethno-cultural issues should be addressed in the church for the benefit of the majority of the members.

Analysis of the Focus Groups

Through the use of the focus groups, the questions asked were refined and clarified. One item that became immediately clear was how one perceived other Koreans and self were very different for some people. So instead of asking how they think others behave, a need for an additional question that asks personal preference in church selection was recognized.

Many reasons for the existence of the English-speaking Korean-American church were discussed in the focus groups. They were comfort zone, outreach to Korean-Americans and others. These were collected and incorporated into the survey.[95] It was also learned through the focus groups that seeing Korean face was very important for a lot of Koreans to feel at home. To understand the relationship between culture and ethnicity, an appropriate question was included in the survey.

From the beginning, because of past experience, there was a concern about whether the English-speaking Koreans would admit to ethnic comfort zone as the most important factor in church choice. Therefore, it was decided that a series of questions specifically asking participants' valuing of certain ethno-cultural elements was formulated. These ranged from how personally important is the preservation of the mother tongue to the culture and to the ethnicity of the members. Questions were formulated so that the respondents would be able to choose from a scale of one to five in the degree of importance.

From the focus groups, it appeared that the participants seemed to think of Western cultural

---

[95] See Appendix One.

practices as Christian and Korean practices as non-Christian. A question was formulated to study how the congregation has been affected by the assumption of the Western culture as the norm for Christians.

Since the responses from the focus group participants on the definition of multiethnic church had been varied and having realized that outward racial appearance, rather than one's cultural make-up, seems to dictate how one perceives others, a list of ethnic composition considerations was drafted to see where people draw the line in deciding when a church becomes multiethnic. To make the respondents think more carefully, a multiracial Messianic Hebrew congregation was included as an example.

Survey Questionnaire

A total of 23 questions was included in the survey questionnaire. Several questions required multiple responses. It was estimated that the survey would only require 20 to 30 minutes to complete. The first draft of the survey questionnaire was tested with a group of people to ensure clarity and also to elicit further comments and suggestions. Several comments were made and appropriate corrections were made. Having completed the second draft of the survey, a copy was sent to both project advisors at Princeton Theological Seminary for further review. The proposed survey was returned with a request from the advisors to write each question the specific kind of information sought and how the question is designed to elicit the appropriate response. While answering these questions for each of the survey questions, several additional flaws were discovered and corrected. Having received approval from the advisors, the survey was administered to the whole congregation. About 200 forms were distributed on Sunday and 60 forms were mailed to people who were not in church that particular Sunday. Within two weeks 103 survey forms were returned through mail.

It was found that the 103 respondents who returned the completed survey forms more or less accurately reflect the composition of the congregation. The respondents were 55 percent female and 45 percent male, which is a reverse of the slight male majority of the congregation. Among the singles in the congregation, 57 percent are males. However, among the single respondents, males accounted for only 34 percent. About 15 percent of the respondents were non-Koreans which is about the right percentage of non-Koreans in the congregation. Married respondents were about 57 percent which reflects their proportion in the congregation. Of the married respondents, 69 percent were with at least one child. Also, among the married respondents, 19 percent were shown to be intermarried which is about the right percentage of intermarried members. It is worth to note that about half of the intermarried couples in the English-speaking congregation are between first-generation female members and Caucasian males. As far as the language proficiency is concerned, 79 percent of the respondents regarded themselves as more proficient in English whereas 14 percent felt that they were equally proficient in Korean and English. Only 7 percent of the respondents believed that they were more proficient in Korean.

Evaluation

A panel of judges who differed in their views on ethnic ministry was asked to give opinion on the survey results. One particular discrepancy that immediately became the focus of debate was the respondents' perception of other English-speaking Korean-Americans as looking at ethnicity first in church selection and their own (an overwhelming majority) choices of preaching and doctrine. A conference was called to review the data with the advisors. Both advisors also focused on the peculiarity of the discrepancy of reasons for church selection among the respondents. When other data in the survey were analyzed, they seem to point that those who deny their ethno-consciousness, also look at ethnicity first. The next two chapters will analyze this phenomenon in detail and attempt to provide a plausible hypothesis to explain this apparent denial of personal desire for an ethnic comfort zone.

section three

the misfit

chapter five

mind splitters

Ethnicity and Church Selection

The Gap

When the respondents attending the English-speaking congregation of the Korean Central Presbyterian Church were asked, "What do you think most English-speaking Korean-Americans first look for in a church when deciding on one?" 44 percent answered "ethnicity". The percentage is even higher among English-speaking Korean respondents (63%).[96] These results seem to support the stated working theory.

However, only 18 percent of these same respondents acknowledged they look at ethnicity first when choosing a church.[97] They claimed the quality of sermon (42%) and doctrine (24%) as the main initial considerations. Looked at alone, this question seems to negate the stated working theory.

The strong divergence between the answers to these two questions was totally unexpected and intrigued many, including the faculty advisors. In essence, 42 percent of the respondents said they first gather information on the best English-speaking

---

[96] The English-speaking Korean respondents exclude the bilinguals who perceived themselves as more proficient in Korean and non-Koreans.

[97] Among the English-speaking Korean respondents, 21% said that they look at ethnicity first in church selection.

preachers in Northern Virginia (whether black, white, Korean or otherwise) before looking at anything else when selecting a church. In the same manner, 24 percent of the respondents seem to be claiming that either they first consider all Presbyterian churches or churches that best represent their theological views, then look at other considerations. In other words, the respondents claimed they first look at spiritual aspects (i.e. sermons and doctrine) of a prospective church before considering psycho-social aspects, such as ethnicity, age, and programs.

These self-identified initial motivations are in harmony with a survey conducted by Korean-American scholars concerning the reasons and perceived benefits of church attendance expressed by Korean-speaking churchgoers in the United States. According to the data provided by Drs. Won Moo Hurh and Kwang Chung Kim, most respondents expressed their primary motive for attending church as religious (about 60%), their secondary motive as psychological (about 20%), and tertiary motives as social (about 5%).[98]

However, when Hurh and Kim asked a similar question with different wording, the results were reversed, showing dichotomy that parallel the study in this report:

> We asked another question that concerns the function of the ethnic church and also serves to check the reliability of the previous questions: What would be the advantages and

---

[98] Won Moo Hurh and Kwang Chung Kim, *Korean Immigrants in America: A Structural Analysis of Ethnic Confinement and Adhesive Adaptation* (Associated University Presses, 1984), 130.

disadvantages of attending church?" …Comparing these reasons with the ranked motives for attending church, we noticed discrepant patterns. The religious motive predominates overall the other reasons for attending church but not in terms of the benefit or advantage gained by attending church. The psychological motive ("peace of mind") was the second important reason for attending church but is the foremost advantageous aspect of attending church. Interestingly, the least important motive for attending church—the social motive ("meeting people")—turns out to be the second important advantage gained by attending church.[99]

The majority of respondents in Hurh and Kim's study seem to indicate they regard spiritual reasons as the most important *motives* for church attendance but psycho-social reasons as the most import *benefits*. Likewise, when a group of English-speaking respondents were asked about their first consideration in church selection, the greatest portion of them (66%) gave spiritual reasons, however, when the same question was asked to describe other English-speaking Koreans, psycho-social reasons were given as most prevalent (75%).[100] The precise relationship between

---

[99] Won Moo Hurh and Kwang Chung Kim, *Korean Immigrants in America: A Structural Analysis of Ethnic Confinement and Adhesive Adaptation* (Associated University Presses, 1984), 130-131.

[100] The two spiritual factors in church selection were "quality of sermons" (42%) and "doctrine" (24%). The psychosocial factors

these results and those from the study of Hurh and Kim is hard to assess. What is clear, however, is that there is a gap in people's minds between the spiritual or ideal and the psychosocial or existential needs.

Possible Explanations for the Gap

Explanation One: Ethnicity is a Given

One possible explanation for the discrepancy in English-speaking Koreans' views of others' motivation for church selection and their own is that many of the respondents do not think consciously about ethnicity when selecting a church, because for them ethnicity is a given. Attending a Korean-American church is almost automatic. Since they are accustomed to thinking about sermons and the doctrine when choosing a church, they put these down as the most important factors in church selection without seriously thinking about other assumptions.

If similar questions were asked of white churchgoers, the response would be similar. Since most whites go to predominantly white churches naturally (most churches are white, after all), they would probably also identify doctrine and sermon quality as the first considerations. It would be almost unthinkable for a white person to indicate ethnicity as the first consideration (unless he is part of a white supremacist church). This situation is so natural; it wouldn't be

---

in church selection were "ethnicity" (44%), "age" (15%), "program" (6%), and others (11%) which were also non-spiritual things such as "style of music" or "church size". See Appendix One #1 and 2

surprising if a similar mechanism were at work with Korean-Americans.

However, many of those who selected sermon and doctrine as the first things they look at when choosing a church answered that other English-speaking Koreans probably look at ethnicity first. This seems to indicate that ethnicity is on their minds all along. In other words, they are very ethnically conscious about church selection but for some reason have decided that ethnicity does not warrant first consideration—unlike the other English-speaking Korean-Americans they know. Basically, what they are saying is ethnicity matters to others but not to them. This leads to the next two possible explanations.

Explanation Two: Ethnicity Is a Non-issue

Another possible explanation is that for most of the respondents, ethnicity is not important. They can be just as at home in a predominantly white church.[101] Again, if this kind of explanation is adopted, one must believe that these English-speaking Koreans just happen to be in a predominantly English-speaking Korean congregation because the sermons are to their liking and they agree with the church's teaching. In fact, it has to be assumed that they examined many non-Korean churches with good preachers and doctrinal soundness in the area and have concluded that this particular church suits their needs most adequately.

---

[101] For some reason, most Asians do not feel at home in either black or Hispanic churches.

This explanation might persuasively explain the attitudes of English-speaking Korean who attend non-Korean churches but for those who attend an English-language Korean church, this is a highly unlikely hypothesis. If it were so, why are they in an ethnic church?

Explanation Three: Ethnicity is Less Important

A more plausible explanation is this: Although ethnicity is very important for most of the respondents, good sermons and doctrine are even more important. They have been taught and are convinced of the biblical teaching that all Christians have a new identity in Christ. They believe they are Christian before Korean-American. Therefore, spiritual things must be the most important considerations for choosing a church.

If true, this explanation begs the question: would these respondents be willing to go to a predominantly white Presbyterian church with a better preacher instead of attending an English-speaking Korean church with a preacher who might not be as skilled as the white preacher? The fact is there are many great preachers in Northern Virginia as good as, or even better than, the preacher at KCPC.

The facts notwithstanding, it may be the case that the respondents have the opinion that their preacher is of the highest caliber and their church the most doctrinally sound in Northern Virginia. If this is how the respondents feel, it may be because of the ethno-culturally relevant ministry they receive from the church. One's preference of sermons is a highly subjective matter. It could be the respondents identify better with a Korean-American preacher because of similar ethnicity, experience and background.

If this is so, it's not the preaching but the ethnicity and culture that respondents first look at—whether they realize it or not. Therefore, the stated working theory has not yet been disproved and the rest of the survey results must be further scrutinized. As it will be shown, they seem to indicate the respondents are indeed very ethnic conscious.

Denial/Suppression Hypothesis

A careful analysis of available survey data suggests most respondents desire an ethnically and culturally relevant ministry but display unconscious denial or conscious suppression of overt displays of expressions of that desire.

Desire for Cultural Relevancy

In the survey, following the first two questions regarding ethnicity and church selection, respondents were asked to identify the most important reasons (both cultural and non-cultural) for the existence of Korean-American English-language churches. Their number one choice was: "to provide a safe and comfortable spiritual haven for English-speaking Korean-Americans" (48%). Other choices were: "to reach out to unreached Korean-Americans who otherwise could not be reached effectively by non-Koreans" (31%); "to preserve Korean language and cultural heritage" (9%); and "to provide a rallying forum for Korean-American social and political action (2%). Over 90 percent of the respondents believed that English-speaking Korean churches exist to cater to English-speaking Koreans; therefore, it's doubtful that members aren't attracted to the church for ethno-cultural reasons.

When a separate question was asked for the most important ethno-cultural reasons for attending a Korean church, the first was "culturally relevant ministry" (50%) and the second was "to be around people who look like me" (28%). The common theme from both data is ethno-cultural relevance.

Why are they at this particular church? The data seems to indicate it's because the church is ethnically Korean. If that were not the reason, why should any English-speaking ethnic churches exist? Without a substantial ethnic attraction, most respondents would have joined a non-Korean church, if only because there are so many more of them. That very few ethnic Koreans can be found in non-Korean churches indicated ethno-cultural relevancy is a primary determination of church selection.

Additional evidence of this hypothesis is the extremely low percentage of Koreans who said that it is not important to preserve: the Korean ethnicity (0%) or Korean culture (2%) or the Korean church (2%). In fact, 83 percent of Korean respondents said that it is either important or very important that the Korean ethnicity is preserved; 70 percent said the preservation of the Korean culture is either important or very important; and 68 percent said that it is either important or very important that the Korean church be preserved in the US.[102]

Another item of evidence pointing to the respondents' apparent preoccupation with the Korean face as an important element in feeling comfortable and a sense of relevancy in ministry is their overwhelming preference for an English-speaking Korean as their pastor (almost 100%). Another startling fact is that no one picked "Caucasian pastor" with Korean cultural background" as their pastoral preference!

It is very clear that the overwhelming majority of the respondents are attending KCPC English-speaking congregation because it is English-speaking Korean. If it were not, they'd probably be somewhere else.

Discomfort with Ethno-Cultural Exhibitionism

Even though the data presented so far point to strong ethnic awareness and a desire for relevancy and comfort, other data from the survey seem to indicate the respondents are reluctant or uncomfortable about articulating their ethnicity and culture in the church. This is very different from what most Asian-American scholars call the "marginal" Asian-American whose embrace of Anglo America is so complete that they abandon their culture or the "racial self-hatred" that is evident in traumatized Asians in America. [103] The

---

[102] The rest said the preservation of the Korean ethnicity, culture and church is either somewhat important or slightly important.

[103] Stanley Sue and James K. Morishima, *The Mental Health of Asian Americans* (Jossey-Bass Inc., 1982), 95. They identify three kinds of cultural Asian-Americans. The first is the traditionalists who hold fast to their ethnicity and culture; second, there are the

respondents are most Koreans who feel very strong about their ethnicity and culture and yet do not want to acknowledge their "Koreanness" in an aggressive manner. It is very peculiar that even though they are Koreans, they seem to be uncomfortable talking about it.[104]

When asked about the appropriateness of certain cultural practices in the church, more people said that Western cultural practices such as observing American Independence Day (70%), Mother's Day (97%), Thanksgiving Day (97%), and New Year's Day (94%) were more appropriate at KCPC than Korean cultural practices and socio-political actions such as Korean-American civil rights (57%), Korean Liberation Day (49%), Koran Children's Day (66%), Korean Thanksgiving "Choosuk" (58%), and Korean New Year's Day (28%). These results seem to indicate that many respondents feel that culturally, the church should be more American than Korean.

As far as evangelistic target groups are concerned, by far the largest group (44%) opted for "whoever attends the English Ministry" as the group which should have the priority as opposed to just English-speaking Korean (30%) or everyone in the Northern Virginia community (25%). This suggests that even

---

"marginal" Asian-Americans who have embraced Anglo-American culture completely; and third are the "Asian-Americans" who are forging a new identity through creative cultural integration. For "racial self-hatred" see Donald R. Atkinson, George Morten, and Derald Wing Sue, *Counseling American Minorities: A Cross Cultural Perspective*, 3rd ed., (Wm. C. Brown Publishers, 1989), 107.

[104] Russell Endo, Stanley Sue and Nathaniel N. Wagner, eds., *Asian-Americans: Social and Psychological Perspectives*, vol. 2 (Science and Behavior Books, 1980), 45.

though they want the church to reach out to Koreans and maintain a predominantly or at least significant presence of Koreans in the church for ethno-cultural relevancy, they do not want to say it outright. Even though the phrase "those who attend the KCPC English Ministry" sounds like an ethnically inclusive term, the fact is that most who attend the English Ministry are Koreans. This is further evidence of suppression of desire for ethno-cultural relevance and discomfort with acknowledgment of that desire.

Moreover, when asked about their comfort level with the church name "Korean", 30 percent of all respondents indicated that they were either uncomfortable or very uncomfortable with it. Of those who expressed discomfort with the name, fully 90% were Koreans. Among all non-Korean respondents, 70 percent said that they felt either comfortable or very comfortable with or did not mind the name "Korean".

Even though the name change will probably not alter the ethnic composition of the congregation, and every newcomer will immediately realize that the congregation is Korean even with a non-ethnic name, the English-speaking Koreans' denial of the need for ethnic comfort zone or at least the desire to superficially "look" non-ethnic is more evidence for the denial/suppression hypothesis.

This hypothesis is also supported by evidence apart from the survey. Particularly significant is that most church members do not feel comfortable when the Korean language is used anywhere in the official ministry of the congregation, even informally. Many feel uneasy about speaking Korean and being around people who speak Korean to them.[105] If a visually impaired non-Korean newcomer would walk into the worship service of the English-speaking congregation, he or she would not know the church is a Korean-American congregation. Sermon topics, sermon illustrations, praise songs, hymns, the English language and other elements are all thoroughly Anglo-American. Only the faces are Korean.

In most Asian-American sociological literature, this kind of Asian-American, who is neither traditionalist (staunch ethno-centrist) nor assimilationist, is identified as a distinct group. Sue and Morishima call them "the Asian American":

>...the "Asian American" cannot be easily placed on the acculturation/assimilation continuum. Asian Americans attempt to formulate a new identity by integrating ethnic cultural values Western influences, and minority group experiences.[106]

Atkinson et al, on the other hand, identify five stages of minority identity development. The first stage is called the *Conformity Stage*. At this stage, minority persons prefer the dominant culture over theirs and deny their heritage. It should be noted that some people stay in this stage all their life. The second stage is the

---

[105] This intentional shunning of the Korean language may be due to their inability to speak Korean well, which is often times a source of embarrassment, or their fear of being labeled FOB (Fresh Off the Boat—meaning a new immigrant) or being perceived by other English-speaking Koreans as too Korean.

[106] Stanley Sue and James K. Morishima, *The Mental Health of Asian Americans* (Jossey-Bass Inc., 1982), 95.

Dissonance Stage in which minority persons go through the gradual breakdown of their denial system. As time passes, their minority culture becomes more appealing. The third stage is called the *Resistance Stage*. In it the minority person reacts against the dominant culture and completely advocates his mother culture. There are those who stay in this stage all their lives as well. The fourth stage is the *Introspection Stage*. In this stage, the minority person begins to feel discomfort with both cultures and begins a journey toward autonomy. The fifth stage is called the *Synergetic Articulation Stage*. In it the minority person finally forges a third culture in which he practices creative flexibility by filtering appealing traits from both cultures. Thus, he becomes an "Asian-American" who is at home with who he is.[107]

Atkinson's view is insightful; however, I see three main categories of permanent stage (Conformity, Resistance, and Synergetic Articulation), instead of five distinct stages in one hierarchy, with two transitory stages (Dissonance and Introspection). If I'm correct, Sue and Atkinson are basically in agreement.

Based on Atkinson et al's stages, the English-speaking congregation as a community, although there is diversity in the individual member's acculturation stage, seems to be somewhat between the *Introspection Stage* and Synergetic Articulation Stage. They are not in the *Conformity Stage* because if they were, they would be in a white church although some may have come out of the stage. They are also not in the

---

[107] Donald R. Atkinson et al, *Counseling American Minorities: A Cross Cultural Perspective*, 3rd ed. (Wm. C. Brown Publishers, 1989), 39-46.

Resistance Stage, because most are culturally very Americanized. Therefore, since they are continually evolving as Korean-Americans, trying to form a third culture by choosing desired cultural aspects from both American and Korean cultures, it is more appropriate to categorize them between the *Introspection Stage* and *Synergetic Articulation Stage*.

Kaoru Oguri Kendis, a third-generation Japanese-American, researched a group of sansei Japanese-Americans and observed that even though they are virtually indistinguishable culturally from Anglo Americans in many ways, nevertheless have retained subtle cultural behavioral elements that they continue to maintain a very "high ethnic" outlook on relational areas of their lives.[108] Virston Choy of San Francisco Theological Seminary expands on the concept "high and low ethnics" and says that many Asian-American Christians feel free to move from "high ethnicity" on Sundays in their ethnic churches to "low ethnicity" on weekdays in the workplace and the society at large to function more effectively without the encumbrances of ethnic nuances in their public life.[109] The English-speaking Korean-Americans at KCPC also seem to change their ethnic "temperature" depending on where they are. For example, at home, many of them eat Korean food, watch Korean videos with their parents, listen to Korean pop songs, and celebrate Korean customs in the family rituals. In the workplace, on the

---

[108] Kaoru Oguri Kendis, A Matter of Comfort: Ethnic Maintenance and Ethnic Style among Third-Generation Japanese Americans (AMS Press, 1989), 6. Kendis distinguishes among the sansei Japanese American the "high ethnics" who are relatively high in ethnic consciousness from the "low ethnics".

[109] This was discussed on a phone conversation with Virston Choy.

other hand, many of them seem to set aside their "high ethnic" life and become "low ethnics". However, one peculiar phenomenon among the survey respondents is that even though the church is an ethnic church, many have rejected various aspects of Korean cultural Christianity and have become thoroughly American. This may be due to their desire to make non-Koreans feel more comfortable in the church or their fear of being perceived by others as too Korean. Whatever the case, they have thoroughly embraced the Anglo practice of Christianity but feel more comfortable worshipping with those who have Korean faces.

Desire to Be Ethnically Inclusive

The survey data seem to indicate that most respondents want to maintain an ethno-culturally relevant ministry but desire with equal strength to include non-Koreans in the church. When asked their personal preference for the composition of Korean churches in the year 2050, 50 percent of the Korean respondents said that they would prefer them to be "multiethnic with a significant presence of Koreans". Twenty-six percent wanted churches to be "predominantly Korean". Only 12 percent advocated "totally multiethnic" (9%) congregations or integration into the mainstream white church (3%).

As mentioned before, as far as evangelism target groups are concerned, 30 percent said that KCPC English Ministry should give priority to "English-speaking Koreans" whereas about 25 percent wanted to target "all ethnic groups in the Northern Virginia community". The largest group of 44 percent said that the church should target "whoever comes to the KCPC English Ministry," which opens the door, no matter how small, to non-Koreans.

A significant percentage of respondents' discomfort with the church name "Korean" (30%) and the desire to see non-Korean staff as assistants are more indications of their desire to be ethnically inclusive. Even though almost 100 percent of the respondents thought that an English-speaking Korean senior pastor would be most desirable, only 24 percent wanted all English-speaking Korean pastoral staff. The respondents who wanted English-speaking Korean senior pastor but ethnically diverse assistant staff were about 70 percent. Again, the evidence is clear. They want both ethno-cultural relevancy and ethnic inclusiveness.

"Dualistic Ethnics"

I call this group of English-speaking Koreans who desire ethno-cultural relevancy but often times shun the mother culture "dualistic ethnics."[110] These "dualistic ethnics" will attend ethnic churches but do not want all-ethnic-Korean congregation. They may practice

---

[110] C. Peter Wagner calls these who need ethnic English language churches "fellow-traveler" or "marginal ethnics." However, it seems to me that among these ethnics, there are two subgroups: one is very ethnocentric English-speakers who desire a very ethno-cultural ministry and another group which I call "dualistic ethnics" that seem to be the larger of the two who prefer ethnic churches but want to tone down or even eliminate ethno-cultural elements in the church. See C. Peter Wagner, "A Vision for Evangelizing the Real America", *International Bulletin of Missionary Research* 10, no. 2 (April 1986): 59-64.

Korean culture and language at home but are reluctant to express them in church. They want culturally relevant ministry but are uncomfortable with overt ethno-cultural displays in the church. It seems that they are "low ethnic" even in an ethnic church. Indeed, the name "dualistic ethnics" befits them.

Andrew Sung Park, a Korean-American theologian, seems to describe these "dualistic ethnics" in his study of the three main "survival models" of Korean-American churchgoers as the ones who fit the "paradoxical model". Whereas those who fit the "withdrawal model" prefer to associate only with other Korean Christians and maintain a "ghettoization" of members and their children, those who are of the "paradoxical model" try to keep an ambiguous balance between their Korean Christian identity and worldly citizenship.

> In response to the dominant culture, Korean-Americans of the paradoxical model attempt to maintain their own culture…Their ideal is to sustain the Korean culture while learning from the mainstream culture. Thus, they live in the polarity and conflict between the two cultures. They belong to both cultures, yet identify with neither fully…*Ambiguity* and *paradox* describe their experience in the life of immigrant marginality.[111]

However, the "dualistic ethnics" differ from the "paradoxicals" in that many do not intentionally strive

---

[111] Andrew Sung Park, *Racial Conflict and Healing: An Asian-American Theological Perspective* (Orbis Books, 1996), 96-97.

to sustain the Korean culture in their lives. Unlike the "paradoxicals" who feel they belong to both cultures and yet cannot identify with either fully, the "dualistic ethnics" identify with the American culture more than the Korean culture. And as far as Christianity is concerned, they have more or less thoroughly embraced the Anglo Christianity. However, they prefer attending a Korean-American church. In this sense the "dualistic ethnics" are also different from what Park calls the "assimilationists" who dislike public display of ethnic culture but prefer attending Anglo churches.[112]

The implications for these findings will be critical in ministerial applications. Unless Korean-American church leaders cater to these sensitivities, many English-speaking Koreans will not feel at home in their churches. Therefore, the Korean-American church will have harder time attracting and keeping these "dualistic ethnics" who seem to be the majority of the English-speaking Koreans. The strategies for effective ministry to these "dualistic ethnics" in the English-speaking Korean church will be discussed in Chapter Five.

Areas Proposed for Further Study

It would be fascinating to study the similarities and differences between the "dualistic ethnics" and what Harvey M. Conn calls "cross-cultural" ethnics" who feel at home in multiethnic churches.[113] Even though

---

[112] Ibid., 95.
[113] Harvey M. Conn, *The American City and the Evangelical Church* (Baker, 1994), 189.

they seem to share their discomfort with the mother culture, they differ in their church preference. It would also be helpful to study the aforementioned ethnics and compare them with what Peter Wagner calls "alienated ethnics" who are happy in Anglo churches.[114] These three groups of ethnics are the three major paradigms which will shape the future of the English-speaking Korean-American Christians. However, it seems by far the largest group among the three is the "dualistic ethnics".

Another area of suggested study is researching the unchurched English-speaking Koreans and see which of the three "ethnics" they identify with the most. The findings will be critical in planning and implementing strategies to reach out to the unchurched Korean-Americans.

My guess is that more single English-speaking Koreans will prefer Anglo or multiethnic churches due to their apparent orientation toward multiculturalism. Among the married couples, however, the English-speaking Korean couples will be more likely to prefer English-speaking Korean churches. Likewise, the English-speaking Korean males and their non-Korean wives and English-speaking Korean females who have strong ethnic consciousness and their willing non-Korean husbands will probably prefer English-speaking Korean churches. Very Americanized Korean females married to non-Koreans will tend to prefer either Anglo or multiethnic churches.

---

[114] Ibid., 189, citing C. Peter Wagner, "A Vision for Evangelizing Real America", *International Bulletin of Missionary Research* 10, no. 2 (April 1986): 59-64.

In the next chapter, we shall examine the survey data to see if there is discrepancy between the aforementioned singles and couples, males and females, Koreans and non-Koreans, and bilinguals and monolinguals in more detail.

chapter six

liminal variations

Singles versus Couples

Pastoral observation found singles to be particularly open to ethnic plurality and often aggressively multicultural in their vision for the church. Among many possible reasons for this tendency, two stand out. One is youthful idealism. Young adults in college and recent graduates are of an age when many begin to hold strong convictions on important issues. In the church, these young adults take to heart what they regard as an undeniable biblical teaching of the solidarity of all in Christ and seriously strive to practice it. However, when they do not see the church actively promote all-embracing ministry, through an apparent complacency or reluctance to wholeheartedly reach out to all peoples in the local community, their idealist outlook often becomes disillusioned.

A recent incident at KCPC illustrates this point. When the former pastor of the English-speaking congregation, Pastor R, left to plant an independent multiethnic church, those who followed him initially were all singles. Even at the time of this report, Pastor R's church is still mostly singles. Despite the exodus of many of those with a multiethnic vision, the singles who remained at KCPC English Ministry are still less likely to hold to ethnocentric views than their married peers, as survey results show.

The second reason why singles are less ethnocentric is because perhaps they do not yet have a spouse and children. Whatever their age, those who are married in the Korean community tend to be more ethnocentric. When Korean-Americans prepare themselves for marriage, many of them begin to realize for the first time that they are different from mainstream America. Korean parents tend to be very active in many aspects of their children's weddings. Parents teach their children the Korean cultural elements in weddings and marriage. Many Korean-American engaged couples face culture shock as they are often taught Korean wedding practices that contradict American practices for the first time.

Furthermore, as husband and wife live together, developing their own family culture, they find themselves exchanging with one another different Korean cultural practices learned in their respective homes. This is especially true when one spouse is more culturally Korean than the other. Most of the time, the wife is more Korean in culture and she often leads the husband into the practice of the mother culture, including the language.

The Korean-American couples' discovery of the mother culture becomes more dramatic as they begin to have children. Even during pregnancy, mothers or mothers-in-law interact more with their daughters or daughters-in-law, teaching them how to nurture the unborn in the Korean way. This is quite natural, as the expectant mother is not experienced.

Once the child is born, the influence of the older generation only increases, as mothers of the new moms usually stay with the couple for a month or more to take care of the mother and baby in the traditional way.[115]

The new grandparents interact with and play with the baby, using Korean terms of affection and Korean learning games. For the first time in their lives, the new parents learn how to use these terms and games, which expose them further to the Korean culture.[116]

The baby's growth brings more education for the parents. The 100th day anniversary of the baby's birth is the occasion for the important *beggil* celebration. The first birthday brings another celebration called *dore*. With their heightened cultural consciousness, they look for a culturally nurturing environment, usually a Korean church, where they can provide their children opportunities to acquire Korean culture, language, and friendships to reinforce their primary home training.

Given so many opportunities and reasons to learn and appreciate the heritage of the mother culture, it is no wonder that married couples are more ethnocentric than singles, despite whose most recent influences came from strongly multicultural college campuses.

Survey results also seem to support the hypothesis that couples are more ethnocentric than singles. Even though both singles and couples in this congregation seem to be very ethnocentric, couples nevertheless tend to be more so. When asked how important the preservation of the Korean culture in the US is for them personally, 73 percent of the married Korean

---

[115] For example, new mothers are instructed not to touch cold water for a month fearing adverse effect on the long-term health.
[116] It is interesting to note that even though the new parents are American-born and raised, many of them do not know how to use Western terms of affection for babies.

respondents said it is either important or very important. For Korean single respondents a smaller percentage (67%) said the same. Also, when the respondents were asked their personal preference for the ethnicity of Korean churches in the year 2050, 13 percent of single Korean respondents preferred "totally multiethnic church" whereas only six percent of the married Koreans agreed. Again, the data consistently places singles as less ethnocentric than the couples.

Although the results of the survey as a whole supported the hypothesis, one question resulted in initially baffling data. To the question, "How important is the preservation of the *Korean ethnicity* in the US for you personally?" 92 percent of single Korean respondents said that it was either important or very important, whereas only 75% of married Koreans agreed. The results are reversed!

The distinction between this and the prior question is that of ethnicity versus culture. For this particular group of singles, it was more important to preserve Korean ethnicity than Korean culture, probably due to a relatively high percentage (85%) of the singles who said that marrying a Korean is either important or very important.[117] Since preservation of Korean ethnicity is critical to their finding a Korean spouse, the results show consistency in this matter. Finally, considering the fact that English-speaking Korean singles are already culturally more American than Korean, and they come the Korean church to be with people who

---

[117] It is interesting to note that no respondent said marrying a Korean is either somewhat important or slightly important. The remaining 15% of the respondents said it was not important that they marry a Korean and all of them were females. See Appendix Two #8.

look like them, this reversal of perspectives between married and singles makes absolute sense.

Women versus Men

As the survey was conducted, it was assumed men would be more ethnocentric than women, given the well-known sociological phenomenon of Asian women's higher tendency of acculturation and intermarriage. Asian-American sociologists such as Sue and Morishima observed that acculturation is directly related to intermarriage. [118] They give five possible explanations for Asian females' higher acculturation/intermarriage rate. First, ethnic females may be better accepted by the dominant society and therefore allowed to acculturate or assimilate faster. Second, Asian-American females may be more dissatisfied with the sex roles accorded to them in the traditional Asian cultures and look for more "open-minded" Caucasian men. Third, Asian families put more pressure on Asian men to continue their family line by marrying within the ethnic group. Fourth, the society's stereotypes of Asian men and women may have caused a rift between the two, especially from the women's perspective. [119] A Japanese-American woman named Jeanne Wakatsuki of Houston tells of her experience in her article titled, "A Personal View of Asian American womanhood":

---

[118] Stanley Sue and James K. Morishima, *The Mental Health of Asian Americans* (Jossey-Bass Inc., 1982), 113.

[119] Degrading portrayal of or lack of Asian men in the American media seems to condition some Asian women to either acquire a disdain for Asian men or a yearning for white men.

I found I was more physically attracted to Caucasian men. Although TV and film were not nearly as pervasive as they are now, we still had an abundance of movie magazines and movies from which to garner out idols for crushes and fantasy. For years I was madly in love with Lon McAllister of Alan Ladd. Bruce Lee and OJ Simpson were absent from the idol-making media. Asian men became like "family" to me; they were my brothers...When I met my blond Samurai I was surprised to see how readily my mother accepted the idea of our getting married.[120]

The survey results confirm that women respondents show less ethnocentrism than men. For example, twice as many Korean men (26%) as women (13%) admitted that they look at ethnicity first in church selection. Furthermore, whereas 37 percent of the Korean male respondents said they come to an ethnic church to be around Korean, only 23 percent of women expressed this view. When asked if they wanted Korean churches in the US in the year 2050 to be predominantly Korean, 40 percent of the Korean male answered in the affirmative and only 17 percent of the women agreed. As far as those who wanted the Korean church to be totally multiethnic, 100 percent of them were women.

The gap between single men and women was not as significant as between men and women altogether.

---

[120] Russell Endo el al, *Asian-Americans: Social and Psychological Perspectives*, vol. 2 (Science and Behavior Books, 1980), 22.

When asked whether the preservation of Korean ethnicity is important or very important, 99 percent of single men and 93 percent of single women said it was. On the issue of the preservation of the Korean culture, 72 percent of single men and 65 percent of females expressed it was important or very important. Again, on the preservation of the Korean churches in the US, 72 percent of men and 52 percent of women felt that it was important or very important. As expected, the male tendency to higher ethnocentrism is consistent, however, females are not far behind their male counterpart on this sample. One possible explanation for this is that people who attend an ethnic church are already very ethnocentric. If they were not, they would not have come to an ethnic church. So, probably we are dealing here with very ethnocentric male and female Koreans.

Bilingual versus Monolinguals

The bilingual phenomenon is not unique to the Korean community in America. However, many have observed that the percentage of bilinguals in the Korean-American community is higher than in most other Asian-American communities. This is due in part to high number of young people among Korean immigrants to America. Research done by Dr. Won Moo Hurh shows this to be true:

> ...the proportion of adolescents [and preadolescents] among Korean immigrants has consistently been the highest among all Asian immigrant groups since 1971,

averaging about 37.9 percent. Data from the Immigration and Naturalization Service show a higher percentage of Korean immigrants in the ten to nineteen year age group than in any other Asian community.[121]

Some have pointed out that the Korean immigration to America is very unique in the sense that it has been primarily family immigration, unlike Chinese and Japanese immigration, which consisted mostly of men. As Kitano explains:

> Unlike the early Chinese, Japanese, and Filipinos, who came largely as individuals, Korean immigrants often arrived in family groups. Thus, even though all of the individuals were born in Korea, the family composition may include infants, adolescents, and young adults, along with the father and mother. As a consequence, intergenerational differences in terms of acculturation, identity, language facility, and coming to grips with the dominant culture, have an immediacy that was delayed for the older Asian groups...It is not unusual to see the following structure in the current Korean community: father and mother, born in Korea, following traditional, old country patterns; elder daughter, arriving with a Korean high school diploma, being more Korean than American; second daughter, finishing high school in America and having

---

[121] Sang Hyun Lee and John V. Moore, eds., *Korean American Ministry*, expanded ed. (PCUSA, 1993), 217.

more American ways than Korean ways; and the younger son, having gone through his entire schooling in the United States, being almost thoroughly American in culture...The mixture, referred to as culture conflict, often causes a considerable amount of difficulty within families.[122]

It may be true that cultural and generational conflicts are more intense in the Korean-American family, but because of the significant presence of the competent bicultural/bilingual contingent in the community (so called the 1.5 generation), the cultural and generational conflicts may be mediated more effectively than those in other Asian groups.

In the Korean-American community, as with other immigrant communities, almost everyone is bilingual to a certain extent. Most Korean-Americans probably feel they are more proficient in one tongue or the other. But because of a significant number of thoroughly bilingual individuals in the community, a comparative study of the bilinguals and monolinguals (English-speakers) is in order. In this section, a comparison is attempted between those who perceive themselves to be more proficient in English and those who believe that they are equally proficient in Korean and English to see if one's acculturation level affects their view of ethnicity in this particular group of Korean-Americans.

The survey data show that bilinguals are more ethnocentric than monolingual English-speaking Koreans. Fully 61 percent of bilinguals believe Korean

---

[122] Harry H.L. Kitano and Roger Daniels, *Asian Americans: Emerging Minorities* (Prentice Hall, 1988), 105-106.

English language ministries are needed to provide "haven" for English-speaking Koreans. Only 49 percent of those who felt that they are more proficient in English agreed. As far as preservation of Korean ethnicity is concerned 89 percent of the bilinguals and 81 percent of monolinguals expressed a desire for it. Regarding cultural preservation, more bilinguals (78%) than monolingual English-speakers (70%) are for it. And more bilinguals (89%) than monolinguals (61%) wanted Korean churches to continue in the United States.

However, when the bilinguals were asked what they thought about their fellow English-speaking Koreans' first considerations in church selection, 22 percent said that ethnicity is probably what others look at first. On the other hand, when the same respondents were asked what their first considerations were in church selection, about 16 percent of them said ethnicity. The percentage did not change radically among the bilingual respondents. But when the monolinguals were asked the same questions, the difference between their perceptions of others (63%) and their own (21%) was very sharp.

The above data tells us that even though on the surface it seems bilingual respondents are less ethnically conscious in church selection than monolinguals, bilinguals are more consistent on the perceived role of ethnicity. In other words, they believe very few people, including they, look at ethnicity first when choosing a church. This is probably because, given the high ethnocentric nature of the bilinguals, they do not think much about ethnicity in church selection even though they almost always attend ethnic churches. In other words, to the bilinguals, ethnicity is given.

However, the monolinguals are more inconsistent in their attitude towards the role of ethnicity in church selection. Even though 63 percent of them thought other English-speaking Koreans are more ethnic conscious in church selection, only 21 percent believed that they themselves look at ethnicity first. This sharp discrepancy tells us that the proposed Denial/Suppression Hypothesis is more applicable to the monolinguals than the bilinguals. It seems that the English-speakers are more uncomfortable about admitting their desire to be with other Koreans than the bilinguals. Indeed, monolinguals seem to be more alienated than those who can function well in both Korean and English-speaking cultures.

Ethnics versus Non-Ethnics

At the outset, it would seem more logical to think that English-speaking Koreans are more ethnocentric and culturally demanding. Koreans will be more and non-Koreans will be culturally less sensitive to the needs of the Koreans—right? When the data were examined, indeed, more English-speaking Koreans desired cultural relevancy, Korean pastors, and the continuation of Korean ethnicity, Korean culture, and Korean churches. However, in the case of authentic Korean cultural practices, more non-Korean respondents believed that it is appropriate to display Korean cultural elements in the church. For example, 60 percent of non-Korean respondents thought that just as it is legitimate to celebrate American Independence

Day in American churches, it is equally appropriate to celebrate the Korean Liberation Day in Korean-American churches. For the English-speaking Koreans, it was only 48 percent.[123] About 80 percent of non-Korean respondents believed that celebration of the Korean Thanksgiving Day was appropriate in Korean-American churches, whereas only 57 percent of the English-speaking Koreans did.[124] Korean Children's Day, which has been observed in the Korean church for most of its history, was believed by 80 percent of the non-Korean respondents to be appropriate, whereas for the English-speaking Koreans it was only 66 percent.[125] Again, 40 percent of non-Korean respondents said it was appropriate to celebrate Korean New Year's Day in the church, but only 28 percent of English-speaking Koreans felt the same way.[126]

It is unfortunate that Korean-Americans tend to shun their mother culture even more than non-Koreans! The Irish have Saint Patrick's Day and the Jews in America celebrate Hanukah, but Korean-Americans are more reluctant to celebrate their own religio-cultural holidays. The suppression of their cultural

---

[123] About 70 % of the English-speaking Korean respondents said that celebrating American Independence Day was appropriate in the Korean-American church. See Appendix Two #13.

[124] About 97 % of the English-speaking Korean respondents said that celebrating American Thanksgiving Day was appropriate in the Korean-American church. See Appendix Two #13.

[125] On the other hand, 97 % of the same English-speaking Korean respondents believed that celebrating American Mother's Day was appropriate in the Korean-American church. See Appendix Two #13.

[126] About 94 % of the English-speaking Korean respondents said that celebrating Western New Year's Day was appropriate in the Korean-American church. See Appendix Two #13.

heritage seems indeed to be very strong among these English-speaking Koreans.

The only other major difference between the two groups is that a higher percentage of non-Korean respondents desired an outreach to all ethnic groups in the Northern Virginia community (46%) as opposed to only 25 percent for the English-speaking Korean respondents.

When it came to the ethnocentric church name, an equal percentage of Koreans and non-Koreans (30%) expressed discomfort with the name "Korean Central Presbyterian Church, English Congregation."

Overall Analysis

The available data point overwhelmingly to the ethno-cultural consciousness of the English-speaking congregation of the Korean Central Presbyterian Church. The congregants seem to want to be with others who not only share the same facial features, but also the Korean-American culture, experience, and life situations. On the other hand, their Christianity is almost identical with the Anglo Christianity, which is quite different from their mother church's distinctly Korean Christianity. [127] Many of them are very uncomfortable about others perceiving them as too Korean in social, familial, and religious practices. Thus,

---

[127] Ethnic Christian elements which the Korean-speaking congregation practices are such things as daily early morning prayer services, vocal prayers, hymns and spiritual songs written by Koreans with a distinct Korean flavor, Korean Presbyterian church polity, which includes non-ordained deacons and female Kwonsa (transliterated "Encourager"), and the like.

in order to provide a home for these "dualistic ethnics" in the Korean-American church in particular, and in the Asian-American church in general, a very sensitive approach to English language ministry must be taken to attract and hold on to English-speakers in the church. The ministry implications are elaborated in the next and final chapter of this report.

chapter seven

third culture

Ministry for the English-speaking Ethnics

The primary concern of this chapter is to help English-speaking ethnics find and preserve a nurturing community so that they would be able to continue to develop a distinct third culture expression of the gospel. This is very important because unless the church provides ministries in which they feel at home, things that this chapter is proposing might not be adequately done.

Therefore, we should not apologize for attempts to "cater" to the sensitivities of the dualistic ethnics, for that will best provide the kind of a nurturing environment that will empower them to take leadership roles in their community and beyond. The ultimate goal is that these newly equipped people, having found a home and security in their identity, would then intentionally leave home for uncomfortable environments to impact the world for the Kingdom of God. Dave Gibbons of Newsong also speaks of this need for a home to empower the misfit to transform the world:

> We talked about the need for a haven..., a place where those who live on the fringe—the "mutants" and the abnormals of our culture—can find a place of safety, a place where their gifts and ideas are nurtured, a sanctuary where

abnormalities are regarded as a means to change the word.[128]

To make this possible, existing church leadership must first be helped to understand the particular needs of English-speaking ethnics. This chapter tries to inform and challenge these leaders about the "mind" of the dualistic ethnics so that instead of making unnecessary mistakes and detrimental policies, they will begin to understand and help their fledgling English ministries.

A Need for More Autonomy

Many in the immigrant church context such as in the Korean-American church believe that American-born and raised Koreans are ethnically Korean and therefore must learn to speak Korean and behave in a Korean manner. This is often not realistic, as culturally, many English-speaking Koreans seem to be more distant from Korean-speaking Koreans than Korean-speaking Westerners such as missionaries and their Korean-born children.

In fact, English-speaking ethnics should be recognized as a new "unreached people group" which needs not only missionaries to help plant churches but also a well-planned strategy to raise up trained "natives' for the church to be self-supporting, self-governing, self-propagating and self-theologizing.[129]

---

[128] Dave Gibbons, *Xealots: Defying the Gravity of Normality* (Zondervan, 2011), 24.

[129] The Nevius Principle which was employed in the Far East mission in the last two centuries included the first three *self's*. The

At first, this newly discovered "tribe" will need support from the outside, especially from its cousins in the mother church. But ultimately, they must chart their own destiny as they are guided by the sovereign will of the Holy Spirit.

For now, many need ethno-culturally relevant churches. It has been argued in previous chapters that the most biblical model of church ministry is the "oikos principle". The home for the majority of the ethnics whether cross-cultural ethnics (needing multiethnic churches) or marginalized ethnics (needing ethnic English-speaking churches) is a ministry in which they can find their "fellow countrymen" both ethnically and culturally (not just the mother culture or American culture but a synthesis or a third culture) so that they can find a haven from ethno-cultural marginality. Dave Gibbons of Xealot speaks on the topic of third culture poignantly:

> Third culture actually enhances a culture's uniqueness while at the same time celebrating the synergy of its fusion with other cultures. Third culture artfully flows in and out of multiple culture like water...Third culture is being able to live in both first and second culture and even adopt an entirely different culture. Third culture is about adaptation, the both/and, not the either/or, mindset. It doesn't eradicate color or lines but embraces and

---

fourth *self* (self theologizing) is suggested by Dr. Harvie M. Conn of Westminster Theological Seminary to promote theological indigenization or contextualization of the non-Western peoples. From the lectures of *Doctrine of Church*, Fall 1990 at Westminster Theological Seminary.

affirms who we are, regardless of differences in ethnicity, culture, or mindset.[130]

Interestingly enough, there are emerging pan-Asian churches and Korean-Chinese bi-ethnic churches along with ethnic English-speaking churches. However, such ministries are scarce, meaning many English-speaking ethnics are increasingly becoming alienated and unchurched.

Not only is there a great need for more English-speaking ministries, but also (more particularly) ministries of which they can have ownership and in which they can be creative in forging a unique culture and destiny. This is possible only when the daughter congregation is given the freedom from the mother church to make its own decisions about developing relevant ministry. The English-speakers must be allowed to make mistakes, to experiment with and test elements learned from both the mother church and the American church, thereby to develop new forms of ministry that better fit them.

This can be very beneficial to the church catholic and even the society as a whole. Multicultural peoples tend to be better able to transcend the narrow confines of both the mother and host cultures because their position of relative objectivity enables them to question many outdated or even sinful traditions and practices that are usually accepted without question within the established cultures.

Again, this is possible only when English-speaking ethnics are free to be who they are and become what

---

[130] Dave Gibbons, *The Monkey and the Fish: Liquid Leadership for a Third-Culture Church* (Zondervan, 2009), 39-40.

they need to be under the guidance of the Scripture and the Holy Spirit. Instead of being subjected to the tyrannies of artificial American or ethnic behavior norms, labels and expectations, they can be liberated from the oppression of criticism and conformity and be "Third Culture". Dr. Sang Hyun Lee calls on Asians to a noble task:

> In the Asian world, we are often criticized for not being Asian enough; while in the American society, we are looked down upon for not being American enough. In the house of God, we shouldn't have to be enough anything—except to be what we are and to have faith in Christ...One of the essential tasks of an Asian American church would be to free up the creativity of the in-between people by affirming them for what they are. The household of God, in other words, has to be a place where Asian Americans can dream dreams.[131]

Having a safe home of their own in Christ enables English-speaking ethnics to explore their creative potential as they become socio-religious "new persons" in Christ. It is indeed critical that more English-language ministries be started and encouraged to be self-supporting, self-governing, self-propagating and self-theologizing.

---

[131] Sang Hyun Lee, "Pilgrim and Home in the Wilderness of Marginality: Symbols and Context in Asian American theology" *Amerasia Journal* 22:1 (1996): 154-155.

In order for the emerging English ministries to thrive, first, as part of their self-theologizing effort, they need the freedom to create their own vision, that is, the freedom to become what they want to become (i.e. ethnic, bi-ethnic, multi-ethnic, etc.). Second, as self-governing churches, these daughter churches must be given the freedom of location, that is, they are free to decide for themselves where they want to take root, grow, and be part of the community around them.

However, mother churches always need English ministries for their growing children who are becoming adults. Many of them want to worship and serve together as extended families. It is a wonderful thing to see generations worshiping and serving together in the same church.

Therefore, it is imperative for the English-speaking congregations within the mother churches to be given the freedom to self-propagate, that is, spinning off daughter churches of their own to plant independent churches to reach out to the unreached in the area while still maintaining the English ministries for the mother churches. This is also important because the ultimate goal of the church is to reach not only the people in the same ethnic community but also other ethnic groups who are in need of the gospel. The best way to reach other ethnic groups is an independent ethnic or bi-ethnic or multi-ethnic church that has a separate location away from the mother church. For even if an independent church meets in the same location with the mother church, other ethnic groups are not usually attracted to it.

This is especially true among Asian-American ethnic groups. Chinese often would not join an English-speaking church that meets in a Korean-speaking mother church even if the English church is independent. The same could be true of Koreans. They often would not attend an English service in a Chinese church. But if the English-speaking ethnic church meets in a separate location away from the mother church, many seem to be open to such a church regardless of whether the pastor is ethnic Chinese or Korean as long as the church views itself multicultural.

The freedom to self-propagate is critical in reaching the unchurched. For example, as of 2012, there are about 20 million Asians in the US including the undocumented. Of these about 4 million are Chinese and 2 million Korean. Out of the 7,000 Asian churches, over 4,000 are Korean and about 1,000 are Chinese. There are more Korean churches in the US than all the other Asian churches combined! If we assume 70 percent of Koreans are churched, in order for the rest of the Asians to have the same ratio of churches, there would need to be 36,000 new churches! The most effective group to do this are the Asian themselves due to their close ethno-cultural affinity to the unreached Asians. As of now, it seems Koreans and the Chinese are better positioned to plant churches for them. Without releasing and empowering English-speaking churches to be autonomous, the outreach to the unreached and unchurched Asians looks very bleak.

Marginal Objectivity

As a people that is more able to transcend religious cultures of both host and mother cultures, English-speaking ethnics can more objectively evaluate different religious practices. Particularly helpful is their ability to identify more clearly unbiblical or sinful traditions or practices in both cultures.

As example, it can be seen in the way offerings are reported in the Korean church. Koreans are probably more generous per capita than Americans. Unfortunately, there may be a wrong motive behind some Koreans' generosity. In many Korean churches all over the world, the leadership lists all the names of the offering givers in their weekly church bulletins. If that wasn't enough, many churches have their pastors announce givers' names during the service. Some proponents of the practice argue that it is done for accountability among leaders and members of the church. That may be so, but most would have to acknowledge this practice is promoted also for the simple pragmatic purpose of compelling people to give more to save face. This practice is clearly unbiblical. In Matthew 6:1-4, believers are instructed to practice their "acts of righteousness" in secret. Thus, biblical stewardship and accountability require church leaders to find a way to ensure anonymity, such as assigning a number to each giver and posting the numbers rather than names.

Just as the marginalized bi-culturals can be more capable than their parents to avoid ethno-specific errors in the church, they might be also better able than mainstream America to see and avoid Western-specific errors in the church. As a personal who's cultural background is a society that is permeated with Confucian ethics (which is, from the writer's opinion, a lot closer to biblical ethics than some modern Western humanistic approach to ethics and biblical interpretation), I am able to see a number of trends in

American Christianity which for an Asian are undoubtedly and obviously unbiblical.

The Western church seems to be undergoing a major crisis of faith. Ethnic Asian Christians, by contrast, seems to be in a better position to hold up an absolutely uncompromising standard in what we believe as truth and not be pressured to conform to the clearly humanistic practices of the West.

However, even "sacred" Confucian ethics must be questioned by Asian-Americans in general and Korean-Americans in particular if it conflicts with the Bible's teaching. One of the areas that Asians must work more on is liberating women from the patriarchal bondage of Confucian subjugation of women. Although, I personally believe in the headship of husbands (maybe I'm too Asian) as loving, self-sacrificing servant in the home (Ephesians 5:22-24), the Confucian (and absolutely unbiblical) practice of giving priority to the husband's parents must be questioned. The Bible clearly tells us to honor our parents, but it does not discriminate between husband and wife's parents.

A related, equally oppressive Confucian-derived error is the ubiquitous Asian Christian tendency to deprive women of their God-given call to faithfully exercise their spiritual gifts of leadership, preaching and teaching in the church. The Asian church must give more opportunity to women to develop their gifts and contribute to the ministry of the church in ever increasing measure guided by the Scriptures and the Holy Spirit. Furthermore, it is imperative that the church actively encourage women to excel in secular politics (to the level of president), business (as CEO's) and even military leadership (as head of the Joint Chiefs of Staff).

While Asian-Americans lead in avoiding Confucian-inspired error in the church, we must equally oppose the Western tendency to dilute the biblical teaching of respect for the elderly and parents. Even in the church, many Christians have bought the unbiblical secular notion that when one turns 18, he or she does not have to honor or obey his or her parents. It is clear from the Bible that the time for independence is when the man and woman are married (Genesis 2:24) and that even after marriage, they are still obligated to honor and obey their parents in Christ (Ephesians 6:1-3) by providing for their needs. This includes companionship, even to the extent of living with them when necessary, instead of neglecting them (Galatians 6:2).

Another near idolatry found in the American church is the veritable worship of the family, probably a reaction to its breakdown in recent decades. There is a tendency in the American church, particularly among evangelicals, to put family above God. In this particular theological strain, it is widely accepted as a biblical truth that one's relationship with God and the Kingdom work must be dichotomized to make way for the family. Thus, the top priority is one's relationship with God (salvation or sometimes personal Quiet Time), followed by family and then Kingdom work (church work or ministry). [132] However, according to Jesus'

---

[132] I was taught this by a campus Bible study leader who was trained by the Navigators. Until recently, I accepted this without question. However, as I studied more about the radical call to discipleship by Christ, I have come to a conclusion that what my Korean mentors practiced and taught about even sacrificing one's family for the Kingdom of God is more biblical than the watered-down American interpretation. This, of course, does not mean that

radical call to discipleship, those who stay home or put priority on their family are not fit for service in the Kingdom of God (Luke 9:57-62). Furthermore, Jesus said that if anyone comes to him and does not hate (relative hate not absolute) one's father and mother, one's wife and children, one's brothers and sisters, even one's own life, one cannot be his disciple (Luke 14:26). Unfortunately for many American Christians, family has indeed become an idol.

The church needs more purity of purpose and practice. Fortunately, those on the margins of society are particularly well-situated to help. We can do so by rethinking many accepted norms of the mother and mainstream churches and make them authentically more biblical, thus formulating a better theology for the church.

The Synthesis

So far, I have discussed some of the more clearly unbiblical practices that are largely accepted without question in the established ethnic and mainstream churches. However, it becomes rather tricky when abiblical cultural elements are involved. In the midst of

---

one is allowed to desert or abandon one's family when involved in ministry. I Timothy 5:8 teaches that if anyone does not provide for his family has denied the faith and is worse than an unbeliever. But when looked at closely, this passage is not asking Christians to put family above Kingdom work but rebuking those who do not provide for the basic physical needs (food, shelter and clothes) for the family. In the end, the Bible is teaching us to do both well instead of at the exclusion of the other. It would be very difficult to separate God from Kingdom work or family responsibilities.

continuing tension between ethnic (thesis) and mainstream (antithesis), ethnics such as Asian-Americans must forge a synthesis that will give them authenticity as Asian-Americans (not just Asian or American).[133] This kind of creative activity will give them the freedom to choose from both the mother and host cultures so that they can realize their full potential as a new people of God subject to neither Asian nor American patronization but becoming liberated and empowered Asian-Americans.

The first task is striking a biblical balance between the Asian communalism which often times causes Asians to be public believers but weak in personal and familial relationship with God and the American individualism which when carried to an extreme causes the dysfunctional "unchurched Christian" who claims faith in God but never unites with a local body of Christ, which is the local church. The difference between the two approaches becomes immediately apparent when one looks at, for example, the American promotion of personal "quiet time" and family devotions and the Korean emphasis on communal early morning prayer services. One of the often-wrong assumptions that many Korean believers hold is that Christians who do not come to church and pray together at 5 or 6 in the morning daily are not spiritual or weak in faith. Among many American Christians, on the other hand, there is a tendency to regard one's relationship with God as very personal and individual and discourage others from "prying" into one's spiritual life. Followed consistently, this philosophy can create in many the

---

[133] Hegel proposed that out of the conflict between "thesis" and "antithesis" is formed "synthesis" in his philosophical paradigm.

"Godless" Christian life due to lack of discipline and accountability.

Not everyone might be able to attend early morning prayer services, do personal quiet time, and have family devotions 365 days a year unless one is a member of a monastic order. Instead, freedom must be given to choose what emphasis suits them best. The congregation could be encouraged to have personal time with God on a daily basis in addition to regular family devotions (not necessarily daily). Even though public showing of one's prayer life is cautioned in the Bible (Matthew 6:5-6), sine it is biblical that there be corporate prayer (Acts 1:13-14), the members can be given opportunities to come to weekly prayer services and on occasion daily early morning prayer meetings such as during Passion Week and/or the first week of the New Year.

Another tension that most Asian-Americans feel is the conflict between traditional hierarchicalism and American egalitarianism in church polity. For example, Korean Presbyterianism often resembles more the episcopalianism of the Church of Rome than American Prebyterianism. In other words, many Korean Presbyterian pastors are often very authoritarian. Together with the ruling elders the Korean session has almost absolute power. When Korean-speaking church leaders lord it over the more egalitarian English-speaking Koreans, the frequent outcome is an incredible conflict between Korean and English-speaking congregations. In many cases, English-speaking pastors and members are hurt by the authoritarianism and the insensitive policies of the mother church. The result is often the exodus of the English-speakers from their mother church.

This tension is even seen at the leadership level. When one attends Korean presbytery meetings, heirarchicalism becomes especially apparent. In Korean presbytery meetings, younger pastors are usually silent. It is often assumed to be a sign of disrespect if younger pastors disagree with older pastors. No wonder English-speaking pastors find more community and freedom in the Anglo presbyteries. Finding synthesis between hierarchicalism and egalitarianism seems incompatible to many. English-speakers overwhelmingly embrace egalitarianism of the host culture, having been educated in the mainstream society.

A related area of tension observed in ministry over the years is an apparent disdain by the ethnics for Western preoccupation with parliamentary precision. Interestingly, this has been the case with both the ethnic mother church and the English-speaking daughter church. Many in the Asian-American Christian community across the generational divide, there is a strong preference for relational approach, rather than parliamentarian, to church polity. As a result, Anglo members are often frustrated by a lack of precision and clarity during board and congregational meetings. The Western imposition of their way carrying out church affairs is another kind of cultural insensitivity, which is very pronounced in mainstream denominations that host minority churches. Whereas many Westerners often practice impersonal and less than compassionate application of church laws to the letter and preoccupy themselves with procedural technicalities and the like (sometimes elevating the Book of Church Order above the Bible in church politics and relationships), many ethnic churches prefer a more communal or family atmosphere type of meetings where there is compassion and love even at the risk of not being strictly "constitutional" or following *Robert's Rules of Order* to the letter. There is a need for parliamentary order in the church, but it seems some combination of Western precision and Eastern family compassion and flexibility is desired in the English-speaking ethnic churches.

Another source of tension among Asian-American Christians is often between those who advocate a Western way of raising children as more biblical and those who insist on the traditional way. Margaret Mead's 1959 film entitled "The Four Families" may be helpful in articulating the differences. She studied four families from four different cultures: India, France, Japan and Canada. The contrast between the Japanese and the Canadian families is indicative of the tensions within many minority groups in America:

The Japanese family is extended; the paternal grandparents live with the family of the oldest son. The baby spends most of her time on the grandmother's back…When it comes time for the baby's bath, the mother hands the baby to the grandmother in the huge tub; grandmother holds the baby close to her body and washes it…the adults perform short religious ceremonies…The children share delicate, carefully manufactured toys. Neither the brother nor the sister can claim to own any toys individually…At the end of the film a Japanese resource person was asked what characteristics were socialized into Japanese children. She answered that they should become docile, gentle, obedient, submissive and dependent...Now look at the Canadian family. What immediately strikes us is the children in this nuclear family are encouraged to develop self-sufficiency, self-reliance and independence. Each child has his or her toys and is taught to respect the other's property rights...he [the child] is admonished not to be a crybaby. In addition, the religious ceremony of saying grace before the meal is performed not by a parent but by one of the children. Most interesting is the baby's bath. The ritual is performed with great efficiency. It seems almost a medical event as the baby's nose and ears are painfully probed with cotton swabs. Rather than being in the tub experiencing the closeness of a parent, the baby is on her own. Noting that the mother struggles with the baby for the washcloth Mead comments, "Again, the emphasis on independence, assertiveness and the development of will power." While the Japanese baby (like French and Indian children) is breast-fed and put to sleep with a lullaby, the Canadian baby has been weaned early. At bedtime she is given her bottle and placed in the crib. The light is turned off and the door shut. No lullaby.[134]

Just imagine having these two world-views existing in one family! Unfortunately, this is true of most Asian-

---

[134] Brian J. Walsh and J. Richard Middleton, *The Transforming Vision: Shaping a Christian World View* (InterVarsity Press, 1984), 17-18.

American families. The obvious tension is between the immigrant parents who espouse traditional way of raising children which is very similar to the Japanese way and their Americanized children who are basically American in their way of child-rearing. Some have even erroneously identified the American way as superior and more biblical due to their narrow and limited exposure to the English-language resources from the American-educated doctors and Christian organizations such as the *Focus on the Family*. An outcome of the natural bias from both groups is mutual misunderstanding and even hostility. For example, traditional families in the church often criticize American ways as enslaving their children with strictly regimented and what they perceive as dehumanizing daily routines, whereas more Americanized families look with horror on how the kids from the other side are left to roam without supervision.

When it comes to child discipline, the tension is even greater. The current trend in the mainstream evangelical child-rearing philosophy is close to the traditional Asian way of child discipline—the use of "rod" (Proverbs 13:24; 23:13) to punish so that children will learn right from wrong. However, many American-born and raised parents have bought into the secular American philosophy of physical punishment as "immoral" or "inhumane" and insist using the "time-out" method without physically punishing the child, seeing disapproval and separation from loving parents as punishment enough. In this debatable biblical issue of child discipline, no one way should be absolutized. English-speaking parents must be given the freedom to use whatever means of discipline they feel is appropriate within the biblical guideline instead of slavishly adhering to either the traditional ethnic way or American way as they forge a new third culture.

Appreciation of the Mother Culture

So far, I have been talking about practices which should be either discarded or modified or partially accepted to be incorporated into the continually developing ethno-American cultures. However, there are many aspects of the mother church that are admirable which deserve full appreciation by the daughter churches. A good example in the Korean-American church is the mother church's zeal for prayer. Daily early morning prayer services, which are practiced by most Korean churches, should be encouraged whenever possible so that the English-speakers could be helped to be liberated from the bondage of private spirituality that plagues the American and English-speaking ethnics alike. Many of them are living a lack of a prayerful life, if not prayerless life.

Many American churches are empty partly due to many of them having been deceived into believing that religion is to be strictly private and personal, and therefore one can have a worshipful devotion individually at home and still be right with God without having to attend a local church. The American utilitarianism saturated the core of many in the church and distorted their view of religion as purely a means to fulfill selfish personal goals rather than serving God and others. By bringing religion out in the public, many Americans could be liberated from the bondage of individualized utilitarian religion. Rediscovering the beauty of communal spirituality is one of the ways that ethnic Christianity can help.

Additionally, a peculiar Korean Christian practice of vocal prayer must also be appreciated. This type of prayer is also practiced widely in many of the Majority World churches. The Western silent prayer is actually of pagan Eastern origin. It became widely practiced after Constantine in the West. In the Old Testament times, however, prayers were always done vocally. Even the Hebrew word for "meditation" means to vocally mull over. The Korean tendency to cry or lament while praying is very biblical. The Book of Psalms is full of these prayers of lament. A person with a broken spirit and contrite heart laments. As inheritors of this wonderful practice, Korean-Americans and others ought to cherish and introduce it to the silent majority, who could use more brokenness and contrition.

We also need to learn from the ethnic communities their ministry-focus on relationship building in the church. One such way is the Korean emphasis on and effective use of the home visitation ministry. Korean pastors are known for making regular home visitations whether members are sick or well. They eat and talk together to build friendship and community. The pastors personally get involved in the members' lives, see how they live, hear their concerns and pray together to take care of the sheep. This is a wonderful ministry method. I have found couples more receptive to this ministry than singles. Regardless, pastors should master this ministry for more effective pastoral care.

The Korean church is also known for their love for the covenant children. Americans have their Mother's Day, which is celebrated throughout the world.

Koreans also have a very special observance: Children's Day. The celebration of Children's Day was a major development in the Korean church and society at the turn of the twentieth century when children were regarded as non-persons, just as women had been throughout human history. This holiday can be applied universally for every ethnic group has children. Korean-Americans in particular should be encouraged to take as much pride in it as the Irish do with St. Patrick's Day.

Finally, ethnic churches in America should continue the mother church's love for celebration. Asians, and Koreans are no exception, love to celebrate. Koreans celebrate *beggil* (100 Days) and *dore* (First Birthday) with much fanfare for their children as do the Chinese. They celebrate in a major way 60th, 70th, 80th, 90th, and 100th birthdays also. Their weddings are usually a big feast. Inviting hundreds of people to weddings is a common practice. I have realized that in Korean churches, the same holds true. They love to celebrate church anniversaries and other milestones and even installation and ordination of deacons, elders and pastors. When an Anglo pastor attended an ordination service recently in a Korean church, he expressed delight in seeing the whole church gathering for a special service with guests, gifts, and a banquet. His reaction to the celebration was, "We, in the Anglo church, have ordination during a regular Sunday service, without any special sense of importance for the office. There is no gift, no banquet, no celebration." We must hold on to what is good and special in our respective churches.

Instead of just following others when it comes to Christianity we need to lead as well. Without ethnic

English-speaking ministries learning from the mother church, all these wonderful benefits will not be handed down to the next generation. A third culture church needs both the mother church and the mainstream church to develop its unique expressions of faith.

English as Official Ministry Language

For English-speaking ethnics to reach their full potential to contribute to greater edification and maturity of the church catholic there is an urgent need to provide a home for them. This means removing artificial barriers to growth and, as emphasized, catering to special needs. One important such area is the matter of language. This study of English-speaking Koreans showed that English-language ministries should be carried out officially only in the English language—especially in public aspects of the ministry. This is due to the discomfort many English-speakers feel about the use of the mother tongue and the significant number of non-ethnics in the ethnic church.

This need is seen not only in the survey data but also in the everyday conduct of church ministry. A case in point is the KCPC couples' ministry. The ministry once included a couples' group with English-speaking Korean couples, interracial couples and interlingual couples (in which one of the spouses prefers speaking Korean).[135] Because of the discomfort and unrealized

---

[135] Because of the relative lack of English-speaking Korean women in the Korean-American community, many English-speaking men marry bilingual or Korean-speaking women in America. In many cases, they are arranged by their parents to meet and court women in Korea, which often leads to marriage.

needs felt by both the interlingual and English-speaking couples, the group eventually was divided in two. Soon after, both groups began to thrive.

A visit to the interlingual couples' group would show an additional dynamic: that English is mainly spoken by the husbands and Korean mainly by the wives. The lack of Korean-language proficiency of the men may be one reason for their discomfort with the use of the mother tongue: Men are primarily responsible for ensuring familial/cultural continuation in Korean society, and public perception of shortcoming in this area can bring shame and division. Therefore, it would be prudent for the ethnic churches to avoid this unnecessary discomfort by conducting its public ministry entirely in English. Of course, this guideline should not and need not govern private interactions between individuals.

For many years, the author has observed many attempts to form English-language ministries within ethnic mother church structures and efforts to plant independent English-language churches. Many do not grow simply because leaders have not taken into account the English-speaking ethnic sensitivities about language. Even more problematic are the efforts of many immigrant pastors and lay leaders to instill ethnic Christianity into the "minds" of the American-born and raised ethnics by forcibly promoting ministries in their mother tongue. None of these ministries, to my knowledge, has lasted. Seeing this, other pastors have tried to compromise with weekly bilingual services. Unfortunately, bilingual and simultaneous translation services, with the exception of occasion special services for the two congregations to worship together, tend to alienate both the immigrants and the English-speakers alike. Furthermore, for bilinguals, the regularly bilingual services are a mind-splitting experience and non-ethnics often can feel they are guests or foreigners in a strictly ethnic church. Thus, this kind of regular ministry approach is strongly discouraged.

Paul's words in I Corinthians 10:31-33 illustrate the wisdom and necessity of being sensitive to the needs of many:

So, whether you eat or drink or whatever you do, do it all for the glory of God. Do not cause anyone to stumble, whether Jews, Greeks or the church of God—even as I try to please everybody in every way. For I am not seeking my own good but the good of many, so that they may be saved.

Biblical sensitivity is to be practiced in the details. The right ministry approach for the dualistic ethnics might include refraining from using bilingual Bibles or bulletins. The mere display of written mother language tends to send a strong message that the church is for the ethnics only and therefore might give an unintended impression that non-ethnics are either temporary guests or not really welcome. Moreover, we have seen in the survey results, it is mainly the English-speaking Koreans rather than the non-Koreans who most dislike the use of the Korean language.

Even the singing of ethnic songs should be discouraged. It is interesting to note that dualistic ethnics will tolerate songs sung in languages such as Spanish but not their mother tongue. The exception to this rule would be again cases in which there is a special service to bring together the two congregations to help families to worship together.

An issue related to the sole use of English in the English-speaking churches is the language qualification of the English ministry pastor. The writer is of the opinion that selection of a pastor with the right language skill is crucial to the effectiveness and growth of the English-speaking churches and ministries. Of course, the most important qualifications for the pastoral office should be spirituality, general ministerial competence and character. However, we must also not overlook the fact that English ministry pastors who lack proficiency in the English language will find ministering to dualistic ethnics more difficult. Therefore, it is suggested that those ethnics who are proficient in English as native speakers (whether monolingual or bilingual) must be encouraged to go into ministry.

A Need for Ethnic Inclusiveness

As has been seen in the survey results, even in an ethnically strong English-speaking congregation, a significant percentage of both ethnics and non-ethnics felt uncomfortable about the ethnic name of the church. A name may not change the perception of ethnics and non-ethnics about the ethnicity of the church. However, it's a matter of comfort for the church members. Following the pattern observed above, it is the English-speaking ethnics as a group who seem to feel most uneasy about the ethnic name of the church. And, if they do not feel at home, the oikos principle cannot be adequately implemented.

It is strongly suggested that church names be changed to non-ethnic ones where effective ethnic ministry is desired. In order to make it easier for others who are looking for an ethno-culturally relevant ministry, however, either the pastor's ethnic name should be included in all official church publications and advertisements so that ethnics who are looking for a particular church could identify it easily.

For the church vision statement, more inclusive language should be adopted even though most people who will be attracted to the ministry are English-speaking ethnics. Again, it's the ethnics, not the non-ethnics in the church, who feel more uncomfortable about the explicit display of ethnic elements in the church.

If loss of ministry focus is the concern, KCPC's example may be helpful. When the church decided to change the vision statement to be more inclusive, many in the leadership were fearful that the church would become too general without maintaining its special outreach focus. Even though inclusiveness was encouraged, it was felt that KCPC's vision and mission were not for totally multiethnic ministry. So, to articulate this special mission, a short historical sketch was included alongside the vision statement so that everyone would know who began the ministry and for what reason. These changes may be superficial, but dualistic ethnics seem to appreciate actions that help them not to appear too ethno-centric.

Another consideration that seems very important to an overwhelming majority of English-speaking respondents is diversity among the pastoral staff. They seem to want an English-speaking ethnic senior pastor who can give them culturally relevant pastoral care.

However, at the same time, they desire to see non-ethnic assistant pastors in the church so that the church would look inclusive. It has been observed in the ministry that even though there have been many non-ethnic pastoral interns and pastors called by the church in the past, there have been many instances in which many members could not connect well with them. Even non-ethnics seldom utilized their pastoral services. So, the most plausible explanation for their wanting a diverse pastoral team is not to receive pastoral care per se but to not look too ethno-centric.

The Vision

It has been argued that one of the important reasons for establishing and maintaining English language ministries and churches for Asian-Americans in general, and Korean-Americans in particular, is to provide a home for them where they can be safely nurtured to develop their creative potential effectively as a new people. But that is not the ultimate goal. The ultimate goal is not to preserve minority ethnicity and culture in America, although it might be an important one. However, the chief purpose of nurturing a special ethno-cultural group is that they be equipped to be used by God in a very specific way where others would be less than effective.

The ultimate goal for minority groups, such as the Korean-American Christians, is that they move out of their comfort zones. Having found a home and security as Korean-American Christians, they are to go into environments in which they intentionally become pilgrims in a foreign land to reach out to the alienated and the misfits in America and the world for Christ.

Asian-Americans are the first mission target group that Korean-Americans should focus on. With the exception of Korean-Americans, Asian-Americans are more or less unchurched.[136] They have become one of the most unreached people groups in America and the world. Korean-American Christians have the responsibility to be witnesses not only in "Jerusalem" (the Korean-American community) but in "Judea and Samaria" as well. Their "Samaritans" are Asian-Americans.

A related obligation for Korean-Americans with their high educational background, economic prosperity, fervor for evangelism, and strong respect for the Bible, is working with fellow American Christians to contribute to biblical scholarship and bringing a spiritual awakening in America. However, before this can be accomplished, Korean-Americans must do one major item of homework: develop a zeal

---

[136] According to 2009 data, out of about 7,000 Asian-American churches in the US, there were about 4,000 Korean-American churches, more than all the other Asian-American churches combined. The next numerous are the Chinese-American churches with a little over 1,000. What happens to the Korean-American church will probably affect the rest of the Asian-American Christians. Asian-American seminary graduates are also overwhelmingly Korean. A consequence of such numerical strength can be seen in the number of pastors that Korean-American churches provide for English-speaking Asian churches in the US. This means, Korean-American spirituality will undoubtedly affect the future of the Asian-American church. See http://l2foundation.org/2009/how-many-asian-american-churches-in-the-usa (accessed January 9, 2014).

for social responsibility and racial reconciliation. Koreans having begun to strengthen these areas which still need improvement, I pray that they will become an integral part of reshaping American Christianity and eventually the church catholic.

After centuries of Western imperialism, many in the Majority World have rejected the gospel as the white men's religion. Christianity is seen as subverting their culture and souls. White-faced Christianity has increasingly become a hindrance to the propagation of the good news of Jesus Christ in many deprived areas of the world. On the other and, Asians are making inroads, as the more accepted passport faces in the world. Among the Asians, Koreans are especially well-placed for this kind of work, for unlike the Chinese and the Japanese, Koreans do not have a history of imperialism. Many missionaries active in China are calling for more Korean missionaries, who can blend in as Western missionaries never can. A well-known American missiologist once told me that just as the British church ignited the passion for mission in the America church, the Korean church will ignite the same passion for mission in the Chinese church. [137]

---

[137] Many of the major urban free churches of China are led by Korean-Chinese pastors who speak Mandarin and Korean fluently. In the city of Beijing alone, where the author worked as a missionary, the top three mega churches are pastured by Korean-Chinese pastors who are born and raised in China. They are called "Three Jins", Jin being the pronunciation of the Korean surname "Kim". Two of which are very well-known churches outside of China: Beijing Zion Church led by Jin Mingri (Kim Myung Il) and Beijing Shouwang Church pastored by Jin Tianming (Kim Chun Myung). The future of the Mainland Chinese church and the Chinese mission to the world will undoubtedly be influenced by pastors like them.

Messianic Jewish leaders are calling for Korean-American missionaries to reach out to the Jews, who have consistently rejected the gospel, in part due to thousands of years of persecutions in the West. Similarly, Native American church leaders are increasingly calling for Korean-American missionaries to reach out to the marginalized and still oppressed Native Americans.

Korean-Americans are ideally placed for such work. They have the twin advantage of being American (hence knowing the most influential language and culture in the world) and having Asian faces. If mobilized, they can become like the Celtic or Anglo-Saxon missionaries sent out in the early Middle Ages to transform European Christianity.

Korea currently sends out tens of thousands of missionaries. This is a dramatic increase from the less than a couple of hundreds of missionaries sent out in the seventies. This is the second largest in the evangelical world after the United States. They are well educated, fervent in prayer and are backed by ever-increasing economic resources.[138]

The Korean Diaspora is another advantage for Korean missionaries. There are thousands of overseas Korean churches around the world. Korean churches could be found in Europe, Russia, the Middle East, China, North and South America and even in Africa and Australia. These churches can be used as stepping

---

[138] By 2050, according to a Goldman Sachs projection, Korea will be one of the wealthiest countries in the world with a GDP per capita of $90,294, which is second only to the United States with a projected GDP per capita of $91,683.
See   http://www.goldmansachs.com/korea/ideas/brics/99-dreaming.pdf (accessed February 5, 2014).

stones by Korean missionaries, just as Paul used the Jewish Diaspora to evangelize the Roman world.

However, there is one area of weakness among Korean missionaries. They are culturally, ethnically and linguistically homogeneous unlike the Chinese. In other words, due to lack of cross-cultural experience, they tend to be very ethno-centric, and this can hinder their desire to become leaders of world Christianity and world mission.[139]

Koreans' inexperience in the mission field is due primarily to being latecomers in world mission. Because of language and cultural misunderstandings, they are finding it difficult to work with traditional missionaries from the West in established agencies and programs. Consequently, they have been diverting their energies to the costly enterprise of reinventing the wheel in the mission field. A solution to this predicament is the mobilization of Korean-Americans into the mission field, where they can become mediators between Asian and Western Christianity.

Furthermore, in addition to participating in ecumenical and missiological leadership in the world, Korean-American Christians should, and must be encouraged to contribute to the leadership of Koreans all over the world—whether they are Korean-speaking, Russian-speaking, Spanish-speaking, Portuguese-speaking, Japanese-speaking or Chinese-speaking. Korean-Americans are uniquely well placed to mobilize other Koreans to bring social justice and evangelization of the world before the consummation

---

[139] However, Korea is slowly becoming more and more multicultural due to immigration in recent years. It is becoming increasingly more commonplace to encounter African-Koreans, Hispanic-Korean, European-Koreans, Vietnamese-Koreans, etc.

of all things in Christ.[140] By leading in cross-cultural and inter-cultural missions, Asian-Americans in general, and Korean-Americans in particular, will help realize a contextualized application of a passage in the *Book of Revelation*:

> Then I saw another messenger coming up from the east, having the seal of the living God. He called out in a loud voice to the four messengers who had been given power to harm the land and the sea: "Do not harm the land or the sea or the trees until we put a seal on the foreheads of the servants of our God" Then I heard the number of those who were sealed: 144,000 from all the tribes of Israel...After this I looked and there before me was a great multitude that no one could count, from every nation, tribe, people and language, standing before the throne and in front of the Lamb. (Revelation 7:2-9)[141]

---

[140] There has been already one major national English-speaking Korean missions conference in 1993 in Philadelphia. I was able to organize Great KA-Mission Conference with the financial support of the Korean United Church of Philadelphia. Many Korean-speaking and English-speaking Korean-American church leaders, together with Anglo-American scholars and missionaries, drafted "The Philadelphia Covenant of 1993" calling all English-speaking Koreans to rise up and fulfill the divine call to contribute to the evangelization of the world and take part in bringing a spiritual awakening of America. See Appendix Three.

[141] This passage is from the NIV, with one edit by the author: "Angel" is replaced with "messenger", which means the same.

appendix one

A Sample Survey Form and Results: All Respondents

Survey Forms Distributed: 260
Survey Forms Returned: 103

Sex	Male (46)	Female (57)
Ethnicity	Korean (88)	Non-Korean (15)
Marital Status	Single (44)	Male (15) Female (29)
	Married (59)	Male (31) Female (28)
Children?	Yes (41)	No (62)
If married, is the marriage interracial?		Yes (11)
		No (48)
Language Proficiency		English (78) Korean (7)
		Equally proficient (18)
Spouse's Language Prof.		English (39) Korean (6)
		Equally proficient (14)

All (A), Male (M), Female (F), Single (S), Married (Mr),
Bilingual (B), English-speaking Korean (E), non-Korean (N),
Interracial (I)

1. What do you think the most English-speaking
Korean-Americans first look for in a church when
deciding on one? (circle one)

	A	M	F	S	Mr	B	E
a) quality of sermon	19						
b) style of music	1						
c) location	0						
d) ethnicity	45	23	22	19	26	4	40

e) doctrine	7						
f) program	6						
g) age affinity	14		5	9			
h) church size	5						

---

2. What do you first look for in a church when deciding on one? (circle one)

	A	M	F	S	Mr	B	E
a) quality of sermon	44	17	27	24	20		
b) style of music	1						
c) location	1						
d) ethnicity	16	9	7	7	9	3	13
e) doctrine	26	11	15	7	19		
f) program	8						
g) age affinity	4						
h) church size	1						

---

3. Number from the most (1) to least (6) important reasons for the existence of English-speaking Korean-American churches in the US.

The (number) indicates the number of respondents who picked that particular item as most important.

a) To provide a safe and comfortable spiritual haven for English-speaking Koreans-Americans (51)

Male	Female	Single	Married	Bilingual
22	29	20	31	11

b) To reach out to many marginalized ethnic groups both in the US and overseas with

a more acceptable non-Western face (5)
c) To reach out to unreached Korean-Americans
who otherwise could not be reached effectively (30)

Male	Female	Bilingual
16	17	4

d) To preserve Korean language and culture (8)
e) To provide a rallying forum for
    Korean-American social and political action (2)
f) Other (7)

---

4. Number from the most (1) to least (4) important ethno-cultural reasons for your coming to a Korean church.

The (number) indicates the number of respondents who picked that particular item as most important.

a) To be around people who look like me (27)

Male	Female	Single	Married	Bilingual
14	13	10	17	5

b) To be ministered to in a culturally relevant way
(45)

Male	Female	Single	Married	Bilingual
18	27	20	25	9

c) To find my identity as a Korean (8)
d) To find a Korean spouse (3)
e) Other (20)

Please circle one of the numbers for each of the questions from 5 through 13. Choose from the scale of 1 to 5 of which #5 is "very important", #4 "important", #3 "somewhat important", #2 "slightly important" and #1 "not important".

5. How important is the preservation of the Korean language in the US for you personally?

Very Important 5 – 4 – 3 – 2 – 1 Not Important

5 & 4 (66)   3 & 2 (33)   1 (4)

6. How important is the preservation of the Korean ethnicity in the US for you personally?

Very Important 5 – 4 – 3 – 2 – 1 Not Important

5 & 4 (78)   3 & 2 (23)   1 (2)

Among those who picked 5 or 4:

Male	Female	Single	Married	Bilingual
34	44	37	41	16

7. How important is the preservation of the Korean culture in the US for you personally?*

Very Important 5 – 4 – 3 – 2 – 1 Not Important

5 & 4 (71)   3 & 2 (29)   1 (3)

Among those who picked 5 or 4:

Single	Married	Bilingual
29	42	14

*For example, Korean food, traditional costumes, special occasions such as 100 days celebration, first and sixtieth birthday celebrations, etc.

---

8. If you are single, how important is marrying a Korean for you personally?

Very Important 5 – 4 – 3 – 2 – 1 Not Important

5 & 4 (34)   3 & 2 (4)   1 (6)

Among those who picked 5 or 4:

Male	Female
10	24

---

9. How important to you is your child(ren) marrying a Korean?

Very Important 5 – 4 – 3 – 2 – 1 Not Important

5 & 4 (48)   3, 2 & 1 (55)

Respondents with children who picked 5 or 4 (22)

---

10. How important to you is your child(ren) being able to speak conversational Korean?

Very Important 5 – 4 – 3 – 2 – 1 Not Important

5 & 4 (62)   3, 2 & 1 (41)

Respondents with children who picked 5 or 4 (27)

---

11. How important is the preservation of Korean churches in the US for you personally?

Very Important 5 – 4 – 3 – 2 – 1 Not Important

5 & 4 (66)   3, & 2 (33)   1 (4)

Among those who picked 5 or 4:

Male	Female	Single	Married	Bilingual
28	38	24	42	16

---

12. How important to you is the church's role in helping you to raise your children in a Korean cultural context?

Very Important 5 – 4 – 3 – 2 – 1 Not Important

5 & 4 (59)

Respondents with children who picked 5 or 4 (27)

---

13. Which practice or celebration of ethno-cultural elements are appropriate in KCPC English Ministry (A-appropriate, N-not appropriate)?

The numbers indicate the number of respondents who said that particular item is appropriate.

a) Minority civil rights	58
b) American Independence Day	74
c) Korean Liberation Day	52
d) American Mother's Day	100
e) Korean Children's Day	70
f) American Thanksgiving Day	100
g) Korean Thanksgiving Day (Choosuk)	63
h) Western Christmas	102
i) Western New Year's Day	96
j) Eastern (Lunar) New Year's Day	31
k) Korean language class for outreach	95
l) English language class for outreach	93
m) Ethnic cooking class	74
n) Nursing homes for people with special linguistic, dietary, and cultural needs	94

---

14. Write either "E" for ethnic or "M" for multi-ethnic for each of the following congregations which consists of 100 English-speaking members.

The numbers indicate the number of respondents who said that particular church is multiethnic.

a) 99 Koreans and 1 non-Korean (multi-racial)   1
b) 90 Koreans and 10 non-Koreans (multi-racial) 21
c) 80 Koreans and 20 non-Koreans (multi-racial)32

d) 70 Koreans and 30 non-Koreans (multi-racial)59
e) 60 Koreans and 40 non-Koreans (multi-racial)83
f) 50 Koreans and 50 non-Koreans (multi-racial)96
g) 50 Koreans and 50 whites   91
h) 50 Koreans and 50 Chinese   69
i) 50 Germans and 50 Frenchmen   65
j) 50 Nigerians and 50 Ethiopians   60
k) 25 Koreans, 25 Japanese, 25 Chinese and
    25 Filipinos   85
l) 25 Germans, 25 Englishmen, 25 Dutchmen
    and 25 Swedes   78
m) 25 Nigerians, 25 Ethiopians, 25 Zulu
    and 25 Tanzanians   75
n) 25 Asians, 25 whites, 25 blacks, and
    25 Hispanics   101
o) 25 Chinese Jews, 25 white Jews,
    25 Ethiopian Jews and 25 Mexican Jews   92

---

15. Number from the most (1) to least (4) important ingredient in a church which strives to be or wants to maintain a multi-ethnic ministry.

The numbers indicate the number of respondents who picked that particular ingredient as the most important.

a) Diversity in the congregational ethnic
    composition   46
b) Multi-ethnic pastoral staff

                                                             13
c) A congregation which perceives itself as
    multi-ethnic regardless of congregational
    make up   24
d) Non-ethnocentric church name   13

e) Other   7

---

16. Write "K" for Korean and "N" for non-Korean for the following persons as you perceive them.

The numbers indicate those respondents who said that particular person is Korean. The left column is the results for #16 and the right column for #17.

a) A Korean raised by white parents   86   53
b) A multi-racial person with a Korean father
                                           60   38
c) A multi-racial person with a Korean mother
                                           54   39
d) A non-Korean who identifies with the Korean
      culture   7   13
e) A non-Korean who wants to be Korean   3   3
f) Other   -   -

---

17. Circle the letter(s) of the person(s) above who should be regarded as Koreans in the year 2050 as the Korean population in the US becomes more racially mixed (anticipating a similar situation in the Korean community in the US as the Jews at the present wrestle with the definition of "Jewishness").

---

18. What would you personally prefer the Korean churches to be like in the year 2050?

All (A), Male (M), Female (F), Single (S), Married (Mr),
Bilingual (B), English-speaking Korean (E), non-Korean (N),
Interracial (I)

a) Remain predominantly Korean   26
    M   F   S   Mr B   N   I
   16 10 10 16 5   3   3

b) Become multi-ethnic churches with a significant
   presence of Koreans   51
    M   F   S   Mr B   N   I
   17 34 21 30 11 7   5

c) Become totally multi-ethnic   10
    M   F   S   Mr B   N   I
   4   6   7   3   -   2   -

d) Be integrated into the mainstream white church
                                                   3
   N (0), I (0)

e) Exist as a mosaic of all of the above mentioned
                                             10
   N (3), I (3)

f) Other   -
_____

19. What is the most likely scenario for the Korean
churches in the US in the year 2050?

a) Remain predominantly Korean   27
b) Become multi-ethnic churches with a
   significant presence of Koreans   52

c) Become totally multi-ethnic   5
d) Be integrated into the mainstream white church
                                                      4
e) Exist as a mosaic of all of the above mentioned
                                                      13
f) Other   -

---

20. In terms of outreach, which group should have the priority when doing evangelism to incorporate them into KCPC English Ministry?

a) English-speaking Koreans   29
    S (11), Mr (18), B (5), N (3)
b) Whoever attends English Ministry   44
    S (21), Mr (23), B (8), N (5)
c) All the unchurched living in the vicinity   29
    S (11), Mr (18), B (4), N (7)
d) Other   1

---

21. How do you feel about the name "Korean" in our church name?

a) Very uncomfortable and b) somewhat
   uncomfortable
   31

M	F	S	Mr	B	E	N	I
18	13	14	17	4	28	4	1

c) Comfortable and d) Very comfortable   62

M	F	S	Mr	B	E	N	I
22	40	25	37	-	51	11	10

e) Don't care   10

22. Choose the most effective person who can best do pastoral ministry at KCPC EM.

a) Caucasian pastor who has no background on
    Korean culture   0
b) Caucasian pastor with Korean cultural
    background   0
c) English-speaking Korean pastor with little or
    no Korean cultural background   8
d) English-speaking Korean pastor with a good
    command of Korean   86
    M (39), F (47), S (33), Mr (53)
e) Other   9

23. What would be the ideal make-up of the KCPC EM staff ethnically (provided that they are equally qualified)?

a) All Korean pastors   25
    M (13), F (12), S (13), Mr (12) B (4)
b) Korean senior pastor and ethnically
    diverse staff   72
    S (29), Mr (43), B (13)
c) Caucasian senior pastor and diverse staff   1
d) Other   5

appendix two

A Sample Survey Form and Results: All Koreans

Sex	Male (35)	Female (53)
Ethnicity	Korean (88)	Non-Korean (-)
Marital Status	Single (40)	Male (11) Female (29)
	Married (48)	Male (24) Female (24)
Children?	Yes (33)	No (15)
If married, is the marriage interracial? Yes (4) No (44)
Language Proficiency	English (63) Korean (7)
	Equally proficient (18)
Spouse's Language Prof.	English (32) Korean (4)
	Equally proficient (12)

All (A), Male (M), Female (F), Single (S), Married (Mr),
Bilingual (B), English-speaking Korean (E), non-Korean (N),
Interracial (I)

1. What do you think the most English-speaking
Korean-Americans first look for in a church when
deciding on one? (circle one)

	A	M	F	S	Mr	B	E
a) quality of sermon	16						
b) style of music	1						
c) location	0						
d) ethnicity	39	18	21	18	21	4	34
e) doctrine	5						
f) program	5						
g) age affinity	13			5	8		
h) church size	5						

2. What do you first look for in a church when deciding on one? (circle one)

	A	M	F	S	Mr	B	E
a) quality of sermon	38	12	26	21	17		
b) style of music	0						
c) location	1						
d) ethnicity	16	9	7	7	9	3	13
e) doctrine	21	7	14	7	14		
f) program	5						
g) age affinity	4						
h) church size	1						

3. Number from the most (1) to least (6) important reasons for the existence of English-speaking Korean-American churches in the US.

The (number) indicates the number of respondents who picked that particular item as most important.

a) To provide a safe and comfortable spiritual haven for English-speaking Koreans-Americans (42)

M	F	S	Mr	B	E
16	26	17	25	11	27

b) To reach out to many marginalized ethnic
     groups both in the US and overseas with
        a more acceptable non-Western face   (4)
c) To reach out to unreached Korean-Americans
who otherwise could not be reach effectively   (27)

174

Male	Female	Bilingual	English
14	13	4	23

d) To preserve Korean language and culture (8)
e) To provide a rallying forum for Korean-
    American social and political action (2)
f) Other (5)

---

4. Number from the most (1) to least (4) important ethno-cultural reasons for your coming to a Korean church.

The (number) indicates the number of respondents who picked that particular item as most important.

a) To be around people who look like me (25)

M	F	S	Mr	B	E
13	12	9	16	5	17

b) To be ministered to in a culturally relevant
    way (44)

M	F	S	Mr	B	E
17	27	20	24	9	33

c) To find my identity as a Korean (7)
d) To find a Korean spouse (3)
e) Other (9)

Please circle one of the numbers for each of the questions from 5 through 13. Choose from the scale of 1 to 5 of which #5 is "very important", #4 "important", #3 "somewhat important", #2 "slightly important" and #1 "not important".

5. How important is the preservation of the Korean language in the US for you personally?

Very Important 5 – 4 – 3 – 2 – 1 Not Important

5 & 4 (65)   3 & 2 (22)   1 (1)

---

6. How important is the preservation of the Korean ethnicity in the US for you personally?

Very Important 5 – 4 – 3 – 2 – 1 Not Important

5 & 4 (73)   3 & 2 (15)   1 (0)

Among those who picked 5 or 4:

S   Mr B   E
37   36 16   57

---

7. How important is the preservation of the Korean culture in the US for you personally?*

Very Important 5 – 4 – 3 – 2 – 1 Not Important

5 & 4 (62)   3 & 2 (24)   1 (2)

Among those who picked 5 or 4:

Single	Married	Bilingual	English
27	35	14	48

*For example, Korean food, traditional costumes, special occasions such as 100 days celebration, first and sixtieth birthday celebrations, etc.

---

8. If you are single, how important is marrying a Korean for you personally?

Very Important 5 – 4 – 3 – 2 – 1 Not Important

5 & 4 (34)   3 & 2 (0)   1 (6)

Among those who picked 5 or 4:

Male	Female
10	24

---

9. How important to you is your child(ren) marrying a Korean?

Very Important 5 – 4 – 3 – 2 – 1 Not Important

5 & 4 (47)   3, 2 & 1 (55)

---

10. How important to you is your child(ren) being able to speak conversational Korean?

Very Important 5 – 4 – 3 – 2 – 1 Not Important

   5 & 4 (59)   3, 2 & 1 (29)

---

11. How important is the preservation of Korean churches in the US for you personally?

   Very Important 5 – 4 – 3 – 2 – 1 Not Important

   5 & 4 (60)   3, & 2 (27)   1 (1)

Among those who picked 5 or 4:

M	F	S	Mr	B	E
24	36	23	37	16	44

---

12. How important to you is the church's role in helping you to raise your children in a Korean cultural context?

   Very Important 5 – 4 – 3 – 2 – 1 Not Important

   5 & 4 (53)

---

13. Which practice or celebration of ethno-cultural elements are appropriate in KCPC English Ministry (A-appropriate, N-not appropriate)?

The numbers indicate the number of respondents who said that particular item is appropriate.

a) Minority civil rights   50

b) American Independence Day 62
c) Korean Liberation Day 43
d) American Mother's Day 85
e) Korean Children's Day 58
f) American Thanksgiving Day 85
g) Korean Thanksgiving Day (Choosuk) 51
h) Western Christmas 87
i) Western New Year's Day 83
j) Eastern (Lunar) New Year's Day 25
k) Korean language class for outreach 81
l) English language class for outreach 78
m) Ethnic cooking class 61
n) Nursing homes for people with special
      linguistic, dietary, and cultural needs 80

---

14. Write either "E" for ethnic or "M" for multi-ethnic for each of the following congregations which consists of 100 English-speaking members.

The numbers indicate the number of respondents who said that particular church is multiethnic.

a) 99 Koreans and 1 non-Korean (multi-racial) 0
b) 90 Koreans and 10 non-Koreans (multi-racial) 16
c) 80 Koreans and 20 non-Koreans (multi-racial) 27
d) 70 Koreans and 30 non-Koreans (multi-racial) 50
e) 60 Koreans and 40 non-Koreans (multi-racial) 72
f) 50 Koreans and 50 non-Koreans (multi-racial) 81
g) 50 Koreans and 50 whites 77
h) 50 Koreans and 50 Chinese 57
i) 50 Germans and 50 Frenchmen 55
j) 50 Nigerians and 50 Ethiopians 50
k) 25 Koreans, 25 Japanese, 25 Chinese

and 25 Filipinos   72
l) 25 Germans, 25 Englishmen, 25 Dutchmen
    and 25 Swedes   65
m) 25 Nigerians, 25 Ethiopians, 25 Zulu
    and 25 Tanzanians   75
n) 25 Asians, 25 whites, 25 blacks, and
    25 Hispanics   87
o) 25 Chinese Jews, 25 white Jews,
    25 Ethiopian Jews and 25 Mexican Jews   77

---

15. Number from the most (1) to least (4) important ingredient in a church which strives to be or wants to maintain a multi-ethnic ministry.

The numbers indicate the number of respondents who picked that particular ingredient as the most important.

a) Diversity in the congregational ethnic
    composition   36
b) Multi-ethnic pastoral staff   13
c) A congregation which perceives itself as
    multi-ethnic regardless of congregational
    make up   21
d) Non-ethnocentric church name   12
e) Other   6

---

16. Write "K" for Korean and "N" for non-Korean for the following persons as you perceive them.

The numbers indicate those respondents who said that particular person is Korean. The left column is the results for #16 and the right column for #17.

a) A Korean raised by white parents   72   43
b) A multi-racial person with a Korean father
                                                      49   31
c) A multi-racial person with a Korean mother
                                                      45   33
d) A non-Korean who identifies with the Korean
     culture   7   13
e) A non-Korean who wants to be Korean   3   3
f) Other   -   -

---

17. Circle the letter(s) of the person(s) above who should be regarded as Koreans in the year 2050 as the Korean population in the US becomes more racially mixed (anticipating a similar situation in the Korean community in the US as the Jews at the present wrestle with the definition of "Jewishness").

---

18. What would you personally prefer the Korean churches to be like in the year 2050?

All (A), Male (Ml), Female (F), Single (S), Married (Mr), Bilingual (B), English-speaking Korean (E), non-Korean (N), Interracial (I)

a) Remain predominantly Korean   23
    M   F   S   Mr B   E
   14 9 9   14 5   18

b) Become multi-ethnic churches with a
    significant presence of Koreans   44
    M   F   S   Mr B   E

13 31 20 24 11 33

c) Become totally multi-ethnic   8
    M   F   S   Mr B   I
    2   6   5   3   -   -

d) Be integrated into the mainstream
    white church   3

e) Exist as a mosaic of all of the above
    mentioned   7

f) Other   -

---

19. What is the most likely scenario for the Korean churches in the US in the year 2050?

a) Remain predominantly Korean   21
b) Become multi-ethnic churches with a
    significant presence of Koreans   44
c) Become totally multi-ethnic   5
d) Be integrated into the mainstream
    white church   4
e) Exist as a mosaic of all of the above
    mentioned   12
f) Other   2

---

20. In terms of outreach, which group should have the priority when doing evangelism to incorporate them into KCPC English Ministry?

a) English-speaking Koreans   26

S (11), Mr (15), B (5), E (21)
b) Whoever attends English Ministry   39
     S (18), Mr (21), B (8), E (31)
c) All the unchurched living in the vicinity   22
     S (10), Mr (12), B (4), E (18)
d) Other   1

---

21. How do you feel about the name "Korean" in our church name?

a) Very uncomfortable and
b) somewhat uncomfortable
     28

M	F	S	Mr	B	E
15	13	13	15	4	24

c) Comfortable and d) Very comfortable   53

M	F	S	Mr
17	36	24	29

e) Don't care   7

---

22. Choose the most effective person who can best do pastoral ministry at KCPC EM.

a) Caucasian pastor who has no background on
     Korean culture   0
b) Caucasian pastor with Korean
     cultural background   0
c) English-speaking Korean pastor with little
     or no Korean cultural background   6
d) English-speaking Korean pastor with a good

command of Korean	73
M (29), F (44), S (30), Mr (43)	
e) Other	9

---

23. What would be the ideal make-up of the KCPC EM staff ethnically (provided that they are equally qualified)?

a) All Korean pastors	22
M (11), F (11), S (13), Mr (9) B (4), E (18)	
b) Korean senior pastor and ethnically	
diverse staff	62
S (26), Mr (36), B (13), E (49)	
c) Caucasian senior pastor and diverse staff	0
d) Other	4

appendix three

The Philadelphia Covenant of 1993

We, the servants of Jesus Christ in the North American Church, do solemnly make the following covenant with the Lord and among ourselves on this fourteenth day of July in the year of our Lord, nineteen hundred and ninety-three.

Confessional Standards

I. Personal Doctrinal Commitment

We do subscribe to the doctrinal standards of the Lausanne Covenant, adopted by the Lausanne Congress on World Evangelism of 1974.

II. Sending Believing Missionaries

We do solemnly promise that in sending out missionaries, we shall support only those organizations and individuals who believe that the Bible inspired by God and that the Old Testament and the New Testament are the Word of God written, the only infallible rule of faith and practice.

The Korean-Americans in World Evangelization

III. The Unique Calling

We believe that Korean-North Americans are endowed with certain unique qualities that enable them to carry out specific tasks in world evangelization. We promise to do our best to carry out these tasks.

IV. Partnerships

We do promise to work in a partnership of love and servanthood with:

1. The Korean-speaking Christians in North America
2. The Christians in Korea
3. The Korean Diaspora throughout the globe
4. The Non-Korean Christians
5. The local churches and the para-church ministries

V. Ministry Priorities

We do promise to put world evangelization as the first priority in our ministries.

VI. Evangelizing Korean-North Americans

We do solemnly promise to do our best to reclaim the lost English-speaking Korean brothers and sisters in North America.

VII. The Need for Renewal

We believe that North Americans desperately need renewal and revival. We, therefore, promise to be faithful partners in the endeavor to promote the coming of the "Third Great Awakening" in North America.

VIII. Gospel and Justice

We believe that evangelism and social responsibility go hand in hand. We, Korean-North Americans, pledge to do our best to be involved in both as we carry out our ministries.

XI. Reconciliation

We promise to do our best to promote love and understanding between Korean-North Americans and the Christians from other ethnic backgrounds, especially in the inner-city situations.

X. Culture and Contextualization

We promise not to make the mistakes of cultural imperialism of past mission endeavors. We will strive for biblical contextualization of the gospel whenever necessary.

Conclusion

We pray that the declaration this covenant would awaken Koreans all over the world who have received the call from the Lord, to rise and faithfully carry out the remaining tasks of world evangelization. We set forth these articles as our visions and goals for this generation of Koreans and beyond, until the return of our Lord. May God help us. Maranatha!

The Signers of the Philadelphia Covenant[142]

Peter Cha (Professor, Trinity Evangelical Div. School)
Ray Chang (Pastor, Ambassador Bible Church)
Soo Y. Chang (Pastor, YoungNak Presbyt. Church)
Myung Kyu Choi (Deacon)
Debbie Kim Chon (Deaconess)
Hikon Chon (Elder, Medical Missionary)
Jin. S. Chong (Missionary, Church Planter)
James K. Chun (Missionary, Church Planter)
Joanne Chung
Howard Claycombe (Missionary)
Harvie M. Conn (Professor, Westminster Th. Sem.)
Ronald Elkin (Missionary to the Jews)
David Gibbons (Pastor, Newsong Community Ch.)
Hannah Guhm
Yong "William" Jin (Pastor, Bethel Presbyt. Church)
Chong Kim (Korean-Am Center for World Mission)
Daniel D. Kim (Pastor)
G. James Kim (Missionary to Mexico)
Grace Kim (Missionary to Mexico)
Hyung K. Kim
Iron Kim (Pastor, Trinity Presbyterian Church)
John Kim (Pastor)
Paul S. Kim (Pastor, Korean United Church of Phila.)
Young Nam Kim (Elder, Korean United Ch. of Phila.)
William Krispin (Center for Urban Theo. Studies)
Chong S. Lee
Gus Lee (Korean-Am. Center for World Mission)
James A. Lee (Missionary to China, Church Planter)
Jane Lee

---

[142] (Parentheses) indicate how signers have been serving since 1993 to present.

Kyu Ho Lee (Elder, Korean United Church of Phila.)
Soo Lee (Missionary to China)
Ted K. Lim (Pastor, President of ACTS)
Dwight Linton (Missionary to Korea, Church Planter)
Stephen Linton (Harvard University, Korea Studies)
Don Newsom (Missionary to Native Americans)
Barbara Newsom (Missionary to Native Americans)
Greg Y. Paek (Missionary to the Philippines)
David Park (Missionary to Indonesia)
Steve Park (Pastor, Church Planter, Professor WTS)
Leo Rhee (Pastor, Missionary)
Sara Rim (Missionary to Venezuela)
Stephen Ro (Pastor, Church Planter)
David E. Ross (Founder of YWAM Korea)
Ellen J. Ross (Missionary to Korea)
Lisa Shin
David Smith (Missionary)
David Suh
Patricia Suh
Jeannette Song
Minho Song (Pastor, Missionary)
Hayoung Yang (Missionary to China)
Peter Yang (Missionary to Northeast Asia)
Gloria Yi

Plus, two unidentifiable signers

bibliography

Atkinson, Donald R., George Morten and Derald
    Wing Sue, eds., *Counseling American Minorities:*
    A Cross Cultural Perspectives. 3rd ed. Dubuque,
    Iowa: Wm. C. Brown Publishers, 1989.

Brett, Mark G. *Ethnicity and the Bible*. Leiden; New
    York: E.J. Brill, 1996.

Bruce, A.B. *The Training of the Twelve*. Grand
    Rapids: Kregel, 1971.

Coalter, Milton J., John M. Mulder and Louis B.
    Weeks, eds., *The Diversity of Discipleship:*
    Presbyterians and Twentieth-Century Christian
    Witness. Louisville, Kentucky: Westminster/John
    Knox Press, 1991.

Conn, Harvie M. The American City and the
    Evangelical Church: A Historical Overview.
    Grand Rapids, Michigan: Baker, 1994.

_____*Eternal Word and Changing Worlds: Theology,*
    Anthropology, and Mission in Trialogue. Grand
    Rapids, Michigan: Zondervan, 1984.

Davies, Richard E. *Handbook for Doctor of Ministry*
    Projects: An Approach to Structured Observation
    of Ministry. Lanham, Maryland: University Press
    of America, 1984.

Elliott, John H. *A Home for the Homeless: A Sociological Exegesis of I Peter, Its Situation and Strategy*. Philadelphia: Fortress Press, 1981.

Endo, Russell, Stanley Sue, and Nathaniel N. Wagner, eds., *Asian-Americans: Social and Psychological Perspectives*. vol. 2. U.S.A.: Science and Behavior Books, 1980.

Garriottt, Craig Wesley. *Growing Reconciled Communities: Reconciled Communities Mobilized for Wholistic Growth*, Unpublished D.Min. dissertation, Westminster Theological Seminary, Philadelphia, 1996.

Gibbons, Dave. *The Monkey and the Fish: Liquid Leadership for a Third-Culture Church*. Grand Rapids: Zondervan, 2009.

_____*Xealots: Defying the Gravity of Normality*. Grand Rapids: Zondervan, 2011.

Hurh, Won Moo and Kwang Chung Kim. *Korean Immigrants in America*. London and Toronto: Associated University Press, 1984.

Kitano, Harry H.L. and Roger Daniels, *Asian Americans: Emerging Minorities*. Englewood Cliffs, New Jersey: Prentice Hall, 1988.

Krueger, Richard A. *Focus Groups: A Practical Guide for Applied Research*. 2nd ed., Thousand Oaks, California: Sage Publications, 1994.

Lee, Sang Hyun. "Pilgrimage and Home in the Wilderness of Marginality: Symbols and Context in Asian American Theology." Amerasia Journal 22:1 (1996): 149-159.

Lee, Sang Hyun and John V. Moore, eds., *Korean American Ministry*. Expanded ed., Louisville, Kentucky: PCUSA, 1993.

Lee, Young Jung. *Marginality: The Key to Multicultural Theology*. Minneapolis, Minnesota: Fortress Press, 1995.

Matsuoka, Fumitaka. *Out of Silence: Emerging Themes in Asian American Churches*. Cleveland, Ohio: United Church Press, 1995.

Mead, Margaret. *Culture and Commitment*. 1st ed., Garden City, New York: Natural History Press, 1970.

Morikawa, Jitsuo. "Toward an Asian American Theology." American Baptist Quarterly 12 (June 1993): 179-189.

Niebuhr, H. Richard. *Christ and Culture*. New York: Harper & Row, 1956.

Ortiz, Manuel. *One New People: Models for Developing a Multiethnic Church*. Downers Grove, Illinois: InterVarsity, 1996.

Park, Andrew Sung. *Racial Conflict and Healing: An*

Asian-American Theological Perspective. Maryknoll, New York: Orbis Books, 1996.

Pozzetta, George E., ed., *American Immigration & Ethnicity*. New York & London: Garland, 1991.

Sue, Standley and James K. Morishima. *The Mental Health of Asian Americans: Contemporary Issues in Identifying and Treating Mental Problems*. San Francisco, California: Jossey-Bass Inc., Publishers, 1982.

Russell, Letty M. *Household of Freedom: Authority in Feminist Theology*. Philadelphia: The Westminster Press, 1987.

Tran, Tini. "Pan-Asian Churches Emerging." Los Angeles Times, 8 March 1999, Column One.

Tubbs-Tisdale, Leonora. *Preaching as Local Theology and Folk Art*. Minneapolis: Fortress Press, 1997.

Wagner, C. Peter. *Our Kind of People: The Ethnic Dimensions of Church Growth in America*. Atlanta: John Knox Press, 1979.

Walsh, Brian J. and J. Richard Middleton. *The Transforming Vision: Shaping a Christian World View*. Downers Grove, Illinois: InterVarsity Press, 1984.

Warner, R. Stephen and Judith G. Wittner, eds., *Gatherings in Diaspora: Religious Communities and the New Immigration*. Philadelphia: Temple University Press, 1998.

Wuthnow, Robert, *The Restructuring of American Religion: Society and Faith since World War II*. Princeton, New Jersey: Princeton University Press, 1988.

Yau, Cecilia. *A Winning Combination: ABC/OBC: Understanding the Cultural Tensions in Chinese Churches*. U.S.A.: Chinese Christian Mission, 1986.